SEVEN KEYS
TO A POSITIVE LEARNING ENVIRONMENT IN YOUR CLASSROOM

TOM HIERCK

Solution Tree | Press

D1122842

555 North Morton Street
Bloomington, IN 47404
800.733.6786 (toll free) / 812.336.7700
FAX: 812.336.7790

email: info@SolutionTree.com
SolutionTree.com

Visit **go.SolutionTree.com/behavior** to download the free reproducibles in this book.

Printed in the United States of America

20   19   18   17   2   3   4   5

Library of Congress Control Number: 2016951244

Solution Tree

Jeffrey C. Jones, CEO
Edmund M. Ackerman, President

Solution Tree Press

President: Douglas M. Rife
Editorial Director: Tonya Maddox Cupp
Managing Production Editor: Caroline Weiss
Production Editor: Alissa Voss
Senior Editor: Amy Rubenstein
Copy Editor: Evie Madsen
Proofreader: Miranda Addonizio
Text and Cover Designer: Abigail Bowen
Editorial Assistants: Jessi Finn and Kendra Slayton

The timing of the publication of this book coincides with what would have been my retirement from my regular day job as an educator. The decision to instead travel the road to work with dedicated colleagues and to write about some of the ideas they have brought forward has altered that plan considerably. Nonetheless, I find myself reflecting on thirty-four years as an educator and where this journey has taken me.

I do know that none of the experiences would have been possible without the love and support of the best partner I could have, and I am forever grateful to my wife for all that she is and does. At the other end are the best teachers I could hope for as my five grandchildren (Isabella, Leah, Liam, Kaiden, and Wren) constantly provide new lessons and are a reminder that we got lots right with our three kids: Kristin, David, and Shannon. Thanks to all of you for allowing me to grow and learn with you. You are deeply loved and admired.

—Tom Hierck

ACKNOWLEDGMENTS

Although only my name appears on the cover, this book would not have been possible without the support and input of many colleagues and friends.

Beginning with my Solution Tree family, I would like to thank the following key supporters. Douglas Rife has been a tremendous supporter of my work, and his encouragement and belief in my ability to write a book alone helped me to overcome the doubts I had about accomplishing that goal. Claudia Wheatley set the bar high with her view of the potential for this book and challenged me to reach that goal. I hope the book in your hands does the same and more for your goals. Jeff Jones has built a company that encourages educators to find their voice and share it with colleagues. From my first opportunity to contribute to two anthologies through to coauthoring five books and now culminating in my first solo effort, I have been given a forum provided by his vision, and I will forever be appreciative. Alissa Voss has been my go-to person for all of the edits, and her suggestions ensured that good thoughts flowed smoothly. I get the opportunity to share my thoughts in the words of this book and am equally fortunate that the PD team, led by Shannon Ritz and Alison Cummins, arranges opportunities for me to come out and work with you, my readers.

At the outset of the writing and throughout the process, I was greatly supported by insightful feedback provided by Garth Larson, Chris Weber, and Greg Wolcott. They all have full plates and yet never missed the opportunity to provide timely feedback. Some of the strength of this book lies in the narratives shared by practicing colleagues, and I believe their words will serve as inspiration for all who read them. Special thanks to Barry Baird, Kecia Dennis, Kelly Holmes, Bill Krefft, Garth Larson, Kerry Mahlman, Don Mrozik, Elise Nicoletti, Shannon Prosser, and Greg Wolcott. I am also appreciative of the survey content provided by Sean Latta, Richard Payne, and Diana White, who shared some of the data from their "Tell Them From Me" surveys of students.

Finally, thanks to the thousands of educators and students I've been fortunate to interact with over a thirty-four-year career. Your sharing of successes and failures reminds me of the good work that has been done and the remaining work that lies before us.

Solution Tree Press would like to thank the following reviewers:

Jessica Cabeen
Principal
Woodson Kindergarten Center
Austin, Minnesota

Chris Hubbuch
Principal
Excelsior Springs Middle School
Excelsior Springs, Missouri

Eric Ewald
Principal
Starry Elementary School
Marion, Iowa

Sarah Starr
Staff Development and Behavior
    Support Teacher
Carl Sandburg Learning Center
Rockville, Maryland

Tiawana Giles
Assistant Principal
Oak Grove Elementary School
Richmond, Virginia

Shannon Stone
Special Response Team Coach
Kerrick Elementary School
Louisville, Kentucky

Visit **go.SolutionTree.com/behavior** to download
the free reproducibles in this book.

TABLE OF CONTENTS

CHAPTER 3
Targeted Instruction **35**

CHAPTER 4
Positive Reinforcement **45**

CHAPTER 5
Data-Driven Decisions. **59**

CHAPTER 6

Differentiation and Enrichment 73

CHAPTER 7

Collaborative Teams 91

ABOUT THE AUTHOR

Tom Hierck has been an educator since 1983 and has held a variety of roles including teacher, department head, vice principal, principal, director of international programs, sessional university instructor, Ministry of Education project coordinator, and assistant superintendent. This has allowed him the opportunity to see education from a myriad of perspectives that are reflected in his writing.

Tom is a compelling presenter, infusing his message of hope with strategies culled from the real world. He has presented to schools and districts across North America and overseas with a message of celebration for educators seeking to make a difference in students' lives. Tom's dynamic presentations explore the importance of being purpose driven in creating positive learning environments and a positive school culture, responding to the behavioral and academic needs of students, and utilizing assessment to improve student learning. His belief that "every student is a success story waiting to be told" has led him to work with teachers and administrators to create the kinds of learning environments that are effective for all educators while building strong relationships that facilitate learning for all students.

Tom was a recipient of the Queen's Golden Jubilee Medallion, presented by the premier and lieutenant-governor of British Columbia, for being a recognized leader in the field of public education. Tom earned a master's degree at Gonzaga University and a bachelor's degree and teacher certification at the University of British Columbia.

This is the seventh Solution Tree title bearing Tom's name, with number eight in the production phase. He was a contributor to *The Teacher as Assessment Leader* and *The Principal as Assessment Leader*, coauthored the best-selling books *Pyramid of Behavior Interventions: Seven Keys to a Positive Learning Environment* and

Starting a Movement: Building Culture From the Inside Out in Professional Learning Communities, and coauthored *Uniting Academic and Behavior Interventions* and *Strategies for Mathematics Instruction and Intervention, 6–8*. He is also the coauthor of the upcoming *Unstoppable Assessment: Using Evidence-Based Practices to Champion Student Achievement*.

To learn more about Tom Hierck's work, visit www.tomhierck.com or follow @thierck on Twitter. To book Tom for professional development, contact pd@SolutionTree.com.

INTRODUCTION

Pyramid of Behavior Interventions, Seven Keys to a Positive Learning Environment (Hierck, Coleman, & Weber, 2011) is a resource that encourages a whole-school initiative to create a positive culture for learning. In fact, the authors conclude the introduction, "Establishing positive learning environments—collaboratively created, systematically sustained—is focused, powerful work that every school should consider" (Hierck et al., 2011, p. 10). Educators frequently ask me about the translation of these seven keys to the classroom level when I present across North America.

While it's clear that each key is a schoolwide practice (and each is intentionally designed that way), it's essential that the practices of classroom teachers support and enhance the keys. Addressing the seven keys from the classroom perspective, and in totality in that classroom, only further enhances the connections to the overarching schoolwide approach. Additionally, establishing a positive learning environment from the first day of classes allows teachers to focus their practice on those activities and relationships that maximize each student's potential and lead to better student outcomes going forward. Looking at the seven keys through a classroom lens and from a start-of-the-school-year perspective is the first step in contributing to a schoolwide approach. Collaborative teacher teams will further enhance the effectiveness and long-term success of this work. As a result, *Seven Keys to a Positive Learning Environment in Your Classroom* aims to provide seven keys for K–12 teachers to implement in their classrooms to help them create a positive learning environment for all students. This positive learning environment, when developed in conjunction with a schoolwide focus on similar principles, will help deliver optimum outcomes for students and teachers alike.

The Seven Keys

The original seven keys Hierck et al. (2011) identify in *Pyramid of Behavior Interventions* target a schoolwide audience of K–12 and higher education administrators, teachers, special educators, intervention specialists, and counselors. The seven schoolwide keys are as follows.

1. **Common expectations:** School rules, codes of conduct, and mission statements are condensed into a few easy-to-remember, positively stated common words or phrases. Behavior expectations link to academic expectations, setting a positive tone.

2. **Targeted instruction:** All staff teach common schoolwide expectations to all students in a myriad of ways and in various specific settings (in class, in the library, during assemblies, on the bus, and so on).

3. **Positive reinforcement:** All adults working with students make a conscious effort to note students' positive behavior or actions. Timely and specific feedback is critical to improved learning.

4. **Support strategies and interventions:** A written, proactive plan provides a series of strategies that staff can follow when dealing with student misbehavior.

5. **Collaborative teams:** A school-based team (or teams) will receive a referral for a student when his or her misbehavior escalates or academics become a significant concern.

6. **Data-driven dialogue:** Systems for data collection are in place to track schoolwide behavior and academic progress.

7. **Schoolwide system approach:** Systems are in place to ensure that all other keys occur consistently throughout the whole school.

I have amended the keys for application by teachers at the classroom level. The seven classroom-based keys are as follows.

1. **Classroom expectations:** Students co-create and condense classroom expectations and codes of conduct into a few easy-to-remember, positively stated words or phrases. Students know the expectations and the adults model them. Behavior expectations link to academic expectations, setting a positive tone. Everyone in the class uses a common language.

2. **Targeted instruction:** All staff directly teach classroom expectations to students in a myriad of ways and in various specific settings (in class, in the library, during assemblies, on the bus, and so on). Students receive opportunities to develop, practice, and demonstrate appropriate social and academic skills. Students learn social skills in the same manner as academic skills: demonstrate, practice, review, and celebrate.

3. **Positive reinforcement:** Students receive timely and specific feedback—both formally and informally—on a regular basis. Celebration, recognition, and reward systems are in place to acknowledge, honor, and thank students for displaying positive social and academic skills.

4. **Data-driven decisions:** Various formative assessments are in place to track behavior and academic progress. The information collected is specific enough to generate general baseline data and patterns of behavior for individual students. Using these data, teachers adjust, modify, or reteach specific skills in proactive ways.

5. **Differentiation and enrichment:** A continuum of strategies, developed and aligned with classroom expectations, exists to support teachers in working to improve students' individual and group behavior. The focus of the strategies is to help students learn to behave and succeed in the classroom. Alternative strategies are in place for escalating levels of misbehavior.

6. **Collaborative teams:** Grade-level teachers (or cross-grade teachers in small schools) engage in authentic collaboration during designated times to ensure positive expectations and outcomes for all students. A school-based team will receive a referral for a student when his or her misbehavior escalates or academics become a significant concern.

7. **Connection to the schoolwide system:** Systems are in place to ensure that all other keys align with schoolwide expectations. The systems are secure enough to withstand staff changes, yet flexible enough to accommodate changes in situations and circumstances as they arise.

After discussing the precursors necessary for a positive learning environment in chapter 1—specifically focusing on classroom culture and positive teacher-student relationships—chapters 2 through 8 will present each of the classroom-based seven keys in its own chapter. Each key-based chapter will explain the key and its effect on student outcomes and suggest strategies to help teachers implement the key in their classrooms. At the end of each chapter, one noteworthy strategy will serve as quick reference for teachers. Empirical evidence and teacher anecdotes throughout the book will show readers that the seven keys, when practiced and fully developed at the classroom level, enhance sound instructional design and quality assessment practice, create a positive culture, and improve student outcomes.

The Pyramid of Behavior Interventions and the Three Tiers

Throughout this book, I will refer to the pyramid model from *Pyramid of Behavior Interventions* (Hierck et al., 2011) and its associated vocabulary to illustrate how the seven keys can be implemented at the classroom level. The pyramid, illustrated in figure I.1, provides a broad generalization of student behavior and is useful for classroom teachers when implementing academic and behavioral interventions.

The pyramid consists of three zones—green, yellow, and red. The green zone, which makes up the bulk of the pyramid, is where the majority of students in schools reside. These students are predominantly easy to reach (they form positive relationships quickly and easily with teachers and other students) and easy to teach (they display positive classroom behavior). The yellow zone, closer to the top of the pyramid, is a much smaller area and represents 5 to 10 percent of the student population. Such students may be a challenge to teach but easy to reach, or vice versa. The red zone, or tip of the pyramid, is the smallest area and represents 1 to 7 percent of students. These are the students who are the most challenging to teach and reach. Please note, these delineations are based on the students you presently have and are not fixed definitions of idealized students. Some schools may have more yellow and red zone students than other schools. Inevitably, however, the challenge traces back to what is happening in the green zone where the bulk of students reside. Hierck et al. (2011) believe that, although total eradication of problem behaviors may not be possible for educators due to external influences beyond the control of the school, the pyramid model will help teachers manage those precursors of negative behavior that are under their control, helping to create a more positive environment. Regarding the use of the pyramid in student interventions, Hierck et al. (2011) state, "If we believe educators make a difference for kids, then we must also believe that students can move from red and yellow zone behavior to green zone behavior. Our role is to support and facilitate that transition" (p. 17).

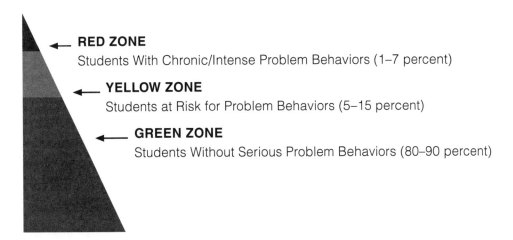

Source: Hierck et al., 2011. Adapted with permission from the OSEP Technical Assistance Center on Positive Behavioral Interventions & Supports (PBIS.org).

Figure I.1: The pyramid of behavior.

*Visit **go.SolutionTree.com/behavior** for a free reproducible version of this figure.*

The pyramid of behavior interventions aligns with response to intervention's (RTI) focus on a three-tiered approach to intervention. In RTI, Tier 1 interventions apply to all students (green zone), Tier 2 interventions to a smaller group of high-needs students (yellow zone), and Tier 3 interventions to the smallest group of students in need of the most intensive help (red zone). According to Hierck et al. (2011):

> *"The support given in the pyramid of behavior model is identical to the academic support associated with RTI. All students, including those with special needs, receive high-quality initial intervention. Tiered supports are then provided to all students . . . based on their specific needs, not based on a general label" (p. 17). They continue, "The challenge for educators is to remember to look at the whole pyramid and avoid the trap of focusing only on the problems at the top" (p. 14).*

Seven Keys to a Positive Learning Environment in Your Classroom embraces this approach of interventions for all students. I will utilize vocabulary from both RTI and the pyramid of behavior interventions when discussing classroom approaches to the seven keys.

A Must-Have Attitude

Creating a positive classroom learning environment is messy, uneven, complex, and necessary for all teachers to engage in. At its most rewarding, it provides opportunities for teachers to have rich dialogue with their students as they collectively work to create environments that produce high levels of success for *all* students. At its most challenging, it creates frustration for teachers as they deal with factors related to demographics, home characteristics, and the existing school culture. At both extremes, maintaining a focus on the learning environment is critical. Education consultant and retired teacher Wayne Hulley states, "The solution lies not in changing the students we have coming to our schools, but in changing our approach to working with them" (Hierck et al., 2011, p. xviii). Prior to his passing in 2014, Wayne would regularly remind educators that parents were sending schools the best kids they had. We need to ensure that all students get the best teachers schools have. It is my sincere hope that this book adds another tool to the toolbox of all teachers to allow them to be their personal best.

PRECURSORS TO A POSITIVE LEARNING ENVIRONMENT

It is in the culture that classrooms build their success. Hierck and Weber (2014b) state:

> *A positive school culture is rich in trust and respect; there is recognition that collaborative processes are fundamental, that there is a collective commitment to effecting the changes that will produce positive outcomes. New initiatives are not repeatedly and haphazardly begun. Instead, depth (of student learning and of staff priorities) is valued over breadth. (p. 114)*

Classroom culture includes the beliefs and commitments made by individuals as they come together as a collective. It encompasses the reality that a disparate group of students can rally around a collective approach. *Culture*, then, is the glue that holds together the efforts of people who might otherwise only be loosely connected.

In my work with schools and districts, I have seen those who struggle arrive at an inevitable conclusion: six months into any new effort, the difficulties that schools or districts face will relate more to the culture than to the established structures. Applying structural change (policies, programs, and procedures) that the classroom culture doesn't support will apparently doom that structure to failure.

This critical shift in focus—from structure to culture—is not an *either-or* proposition but an *and* requirement as teachers build strong cultures that will support the necessary structural modifications to ensure positive student outcomes.

Hierck and Weber (2014b) suggest that creating a positive classroom structure requires some key beliefs or alignments from every teacher.

◆ Teachers value all students and expect all to make significant gains in their learning.

◆ Factors that may inhibit successful gains are temporary obstacles and challenges.

◆ All staff members accept responsibility for all students: students in other classrooms, students in other grade levels, students with disabilities, and students who speak another language at home.

◆ Teachers never accept the status quo; staff members should set students' expectations appropriately and recognize continual improvement as the habit of great organizations.

◆ Staff consider change an opportunity and incorporate all variables.

◆ School leaders and educators view adult modeled behaviors as having the most effective and significant influence on student learning and behaviors.

These beliefs are not beyond the reach of any teacher in any classroom. They very simply require an intention to push past the convenient excuses and reduce challenges or obstacles to variables that highly qualified and skilled adults—our teachers—can manage and utilize in designing high-quality instruction and assessment. Clarity around procedures and expectations help make this outcome attainable, and a positive classroom culture will ensure sustainable positive gains over time.

A singular question should drive the process of developing a positive classroom culture: What is the end goal? If the end goal is that all students are able to make a successful transition to the next grade (or college or career), then subsequent conversations will all center on achieving that end goal. The focus will shift from punitive discussions to positive ones. This step in creating classroom culture is not about lowering the bar but rather clarifying what it will take to clear the bar.

Classroom Culture

When seeking to develop a successful, supported collaborative learning community, teachers must first develop a positive classroom culture. In order to achieve a safe and orderly learning environment with clear expectations, it has become increasingly necessary for teachers to engage in an intentional response to the variables they confront in their individual classes. Why is it that some classes with student populations that are described as challenging find ways to thrive and produce outstanding student outcomes? The answer lies in understanding the culture that exists in each class. Teachers need to examine whether their current culture is moving the class toward the desired goals or away from them. This is a precursor to cultural change and developing the types of learning spaces where students thrive. Progressive and more contemporary pedagogies, strategies, and practices matter, but they do not matter more than positive learning environments built on trust, belief, and high expectations. Furthermore, pedagogies, strategies, and practices will not likely impact student outcomes in the absence of robust and positive classroom cultures.

It is critical to recognize that before cultural change can occur in any classroom, a teacher must desire this change and recognize that there is some value and need for it. My work has led me to schools all across the United States and Canada, as well as overseas, and inevitably I encounter educators who have lost the belief in the efficacy of cultural change. The root cause varies. Has the failure of a structural initiative, the latest in a long list of failures, led a teacher to become disenchanted? Or have cynical leaders and administration hampered a motivated teacher, initially but no longer willing to implement cultural change? Here is what I am certain of: the cynics and blockers in schools today were not those types of people during the hiring process. They oftentimes became these types of people through a never-ending array of new school initiatives, structural changes, and new leader visions, all of which have been implemented with dubious levels of success.

In order to achieve end goals, classrooms need to have a culture conducive to a positive learning environment in place. Teachers who attempt to import structural pieces, regardless of the quality of the structure and the desire to make it work, are doomed to struggle and ultimately fail. If teachers believe in success for all students, they must not relegate the harder, deeper, more meaningful work of cultural change and relationship building to the proverbial back burner.

Case Study: Classroom Culture in 90/90/90 Schools

Douglas Reeves (2003) investigates the characteristics that set apart schools that succeed academically in spite of potentially challenging circumstances. He investigates *90/90/90 Schools*—schools in which 90 percent or more of the students are eligible for free and reduced lunch, 90 percent or more of the students are members of ethnic minority groups, and 90 percent or more of the students meet the district or state academic standards in reading or another area. Reeves (2003) identifies a common set of five characteristics exhibited by the leaders and teachers in such schools that give an indication of their classrooms' culture.

1. **A focus on academic achievement:** A laser-like focus on achievement in these schools includes a particular emphasis on improvement. These schools display student achievement information and exemplary academic work and take pride in student success.

2. **Clear curriculum choices:** The school emphasizes the core skills of reading, writing, and mathematics to improve student opportunities for success in a wide variety of other academic endeavors.

3. **Frequent assessment of student progress and multiple opportunities for improvement:** The school provides any student whose performance is less than proficient with opportunities to improve. There is no evidence of the archaic practice of averaging the results. Instead, students receive the grades they ultimately earn. Classroom teachers construct and administer the assessments. The schools expect that teachers can create high-quality, effective, and rigorous assessments. The consequence for poor performance is not a bad grade or discouragement, but more work with an eye toward improved performance.

4. **An emphasis on nonfiction writing:** Teachers place a premium on written responses for performance assessments. This use of written responses allows teachers to obtain better diagnostic information about students. It also allows students the opportunity to demonstrate the thinking process that they employ.

5. **Collaborative scoring of student work:** The schools develop common assessment practices and reinforce those regular exchanges of student papers to help standardize the scoring across the faculty. The high-achieving schools make it clear that it takes more than "winning the teacher lottery" to achieve

success. It requires more than classroom assignment to determine expectations and achievement levels for students.

Research indicates that classroom culture and positive teacher-student relationships have the ability to overcome the behavioral and academic challenges associated with certain demographic factors. Reeves (2003) suggests, "While economic
deprivation clearly affects student achievement, demographic characteristics do
not determine academic performance" (p. 1). He also implies that it takes more
than sound pedagogical practice or the best-packaged program to break through
some perceived barriers, stating, "The brand name alone of a literacy program is
not the predictor of success, but rather the professional practices employed by
teachers and leaders in the building" (Reeves, 2003, p. 19). University researchers Bridget K. Hamre and Robert C. Pianta validate this with their 2005 study
of students at risk (Goleman, 2006). This study finds that those students placed
with cold or controlling teachers struggled academically, regardless of whether
their teachers followed pedagogic guidelines for good instruction. However, if
these students had a warm and responsive teacher, they flourished and learned as
well as others. These results show that quality of relationship, above all else, is the
springboard to success.

Positive Teacher-Student Relationships

To meet some of the external pressures that often arise with structural interventions, teachers must develop and operate in a culture where all students feel
valued. Teachers must collaboratively create and consistently address expectations
for students while embracing the ongoing struggle of implementing strategies
that work not just for the majority of students but also for those who have not
yet achieved attainment. The challenge of ensuring that all students are reached
is highlighted the more unique an individual student's needs are. This means that
teachers must connect with and address their current students' needs—not just
the needs of the students they used to have or would like to have.

I've worked as an educator in a variety of roles since 1983. Anecdotal evidence
has led me to several conclusions regarding students who feel connected. They
earn better grades than previously; they exhibit higher levels of prosocial classroom behavior, including motivation and participation. They display higher levels
of participation, comfort, enjoyment, and acceptance by their peers, demonstrate
higher levels of social competency, and exhibit fewer inappropriate behaviors. I
have yet to see a student who feels connected (to at least one adult) disappoint. It

is imperative that we take up the charge with more vigor and intent than at any point in our education history if we are serious about ensuring all students make the transition to the next challenge.

Barry Baird is an Australian educator who began his career in the late 1960s. We had the good fortune to meet when I started my teaching career and he was in Canada on a teacher exchange. On a visit to Australia, I asked him to reflect on his career and if there were anything he would do differently. He responded, "I wish I had used humor more, found more real-world or personal links for the students, and understood whole-brain thinking at an earlier stage to help tailor teaching to individuals" (B. Baird, personal communication, January 24, 2016). This list comes from someone whom I would describe as a respected educator who built long-lasting, meaningful connections with the students in his classes. It speaks to the desire to build even stronger connections with students.

Relationships and a Positive Learning Environment

The new three *Rs* of education are rigor, relevance, and relationships. Many academic standards in curriculum guides focus on the first two. The third *R*, relationships, is a concept that many schools speak about in broad terms, but spend less time putting into practice.

One way schools speak broadly about relationships is by setting an expectation that positive relationships will form between students and adults in all possible combinations (student to adult, adult to student, student to student, and adult to adult) as a foundation for positive schoolwide behavior. Honoring this expectation after the initial conversation requires a higher commitment than simply talking about it; if we don't model what we teach, then we are teaching what we model. Fulfilling the expectation to form positive relationships requires active modeling by adults, numerous practice opportunities for students, and a commitment to continue to work with those students who don't get it the first time (or the second or third times) to completely ingrain this skill for those students who need additional assistance. Schools must implement a universal approach in classrooms in addition to simply conveying the expectation of positive relationships to students.

Developing positive teacher-student relations is one of the most effective steps educators can take to establish a positive learning climate and community. When treated with respect, students tend to reciprocate and behave appropriately. Many leading education authors have written about positive relationships with students. Julia G. Thompson (1998) says, "The most powerful weapon available to secondary teachers who want to foster a favorable learning climate is a positive relationship with our students" (p. 6). Alfie Kohn (1996) states, "Children are more likely to be respectful when important adults in their lives respect *them*. They are more likely to care about others if they know *they* are cared about" (p. 111). Education researcher Robert J. Marzano (2003) states that students will resist rules and procedures, along with the consequent disciplinary actions, if the foundation of a good relationship is lacking. Jeffrey A. Kottler and Stanley J. Zehm (1993) believe that students will never trust us or open themselves up to hear what we have to say unless they sense that we value and respect them. I am reminded of the oft-quoted (but anonymously attributed) adage that children don't care how much you know until they know how much you care. Essentially, before rushing to get through the levels of Bloom's taxonomy, teachers need to ensure that they first address the levels of Maslow's hierarchy, and in particular the levels that address belonging and esteem. (A discussion of Maslow's hierarchy and Bloom's taxonomy can be found in chapter 3, page 35.)

Teacher Presence

No matter how engaging or talented teachers may be, they can only have an impact on student learning if they are in the classroom. It's not difficult to see that a teacher's absence from a classroom negatively impacts student learning. Mary Finlayson (2009), in her master's thesis study of a large suburban district, states, "The more days a teacher is out of the classroom, the lower their students tend to score on standardized tests" (p. 3). More specifically, Raegen T. Miller, Richard J. Murnane, and John B. Willett (2008), in a study of a large urban district, estimate that "10 additional days of teacher absence reduce student achievement in fourth grade mathematics by 3.3 percent of a standard deviation" (p. 191). The authors suggest this is a large enough effect size to be of relevance and have influence on policy decisions. Their rationale centers around three significant factors: (1) teacher absences directly affect the achievement of an entire classroom of students, (2) teacher absences reduce the opportunity and functionality of collaborative time, and (3) small differences in the performance of even a few students on external mathematics examinations can result in the school not meeting its annual targets. The focus on mathematics skills begins in early grades, so an absent teacher would have more of an impact on the learning of mathematics skills during this formative period.

The impact of teacher absences oftentimes results in misbehavior on the students' part, particularly among those students for whom the connection to their teacher is critical. It is impossible to eliminate teacher absence, especially when the circumstances are beyond our control (for example, illness or family crisis) or when the system is the root cause of the absence (for example, mandatory personal development during school time or teachers coaching teachers). Thus, it is important that teachers have structures in place, such as the ones suggested in the following paragraph, to help minimize the impact of their absences.

When it comes to student behavior, in my experience it's more often the relationship students have with their teachers than the behavioral expectations themselves that encourages students to demonstrate classroom expectations. As a result, any teacher absence has the potential to negatively impact students, particularly those students who walk the fine line between desired and not-so-desired behaviors. If a teacher is aware of an upcoming absence, he or she may want to talk in advance to the students for whom the absence will be significant. Teachers should let students know that they are committed to lifelong learning and furthering their teaching skills, if the absence is related to a professional development event. Teachers should also review expectations with students for how to treat replacement, or substitute, teachers. Then, teachers should commit to checking back with students and commending them for their effort and support during the absence. This routine will also carry students through those times when the absence is unexpected.

Resilience

Harvard's Jack Shonkoff chaired a multidisciplinary collaboration that examined the connection between resilience and relationships and includes this significant conclusion:

> *Despite the widespread belief that individual grit, extraordinary self-reliance, or some in-born, heroic strength of character can triumph over calamity, science now tells us that it is the reliable presence of at least one supportive relationship and multiple opportunities for developing effective coping skills that are essential building blocks for the capacity to do well in the face of significant adversity. (National Scientific Council on the Developing Child, 2015, p. 7)*

For many students, that supportive adult resides in their homes and is significant in their lives. For those students who challenge teachers the most (and, as a result, who need teachers the most) this role is typically nonexistent or unreliable outside the school environment. In many of those cases, teachers are in the best position to fill that role. While it is clear that time is the most precious resource in schools today, the question educators must face is: If you don't have the time to do the right thing (build relationships and resilience and provide feedback), when will you find time to do it over when your current practices are not working? This issue is really not about finding time—no educator I'm aware of ever ends the day with more time than work. Rather, it is about making the time to do what is right and what will have the greatest impact on students.

Educators can be overwhelmed with managing the many variables (poverty, family disruption, family support for school, and transience are some examples) inherent in their profession. Helping students develop the resilience to manage these variables is a critical part of the work of educators today. As changes in the world outside of school continue, they have the potential to put even more pressure on the world inside of school. While I may enjoy the notion that fifty is the new forty, I am more concerned that ten appears to be the new twenty as I listen to some of the challenges our younger students face. I often share the belief that educators are in the life-saving business, and a study validates that claim. Patrick M. Krueger, Melanie K. Tran, Robert A. Hummer, and Virginia W. Chang (2015) look at mortality rates attributable to low levels of education in the United States, which results in this startling deduction:

> *Mortality attributable to low education is comparable in magnitude to mortality attributable to individuals being current rather than former smokers. Existing research suggests that a substantial part of the association between education and mortality is causal. Thus, policies that increase education could significantly reduce adult mortality.*

Researchers attribute an estimated 145,243 deaths in 2010 to those with less than a high school diploma as opposed to those with a diploma (Krueger et al., 2015). These rates are the same among women and men, and among non-Hispanic African Americans and Caucasians. Teachers truly are in the life-saving business!

Student Acceptance

It is human nature that we may find easier commonality with some people over others. There will be a time for teachers when they are confronted with an exceedingly difficult student with whom they have little in common. While forming a relationship with that student may seem a challenge, an easy temptation in education is for teachers to lament about the students they used to have. Sometimes this extends to the students they would like to have. This wringing of the hands reminds me of the quote often attributed to Socrates:

> *The children now love luxury; they have bad manners, contempt for authority; they show disrespect for elders and love chatter in place of exercise. Children are now tyrants, not the servants of their households. They no longer rise when elders enter the room. They contradict their parents, chatter before company, gobble up dainties at the table, cross their legs, and tyrannize their teachers. (Patty & Johnson, 1953, p. 277)*

It appears that this negative perception of students persists, including from when we ourselves were students! Rather than suffer from *nostalnesia* (only remembering the good about the good old days), teachers need to remember that students in classrooms right now are the very best students showing up at our schools every day. The good news is that teachers have the capacity and skills to add value to every one of them! So, get energized about the students arriving daily and work at addressing their needs through any means possible. Expectations, both inside and outside the classroom, for students are more challenging than ever. Teachers must adapt to students—not expect them to adapt. If the intention is for all students to learn and grow, then the significance of a strong, caring relationship with the key adult in the classroom is paramount. The students who challenge you the most, need you the most. Let's model what we teach and embrace the struggle on the road to building a positive learning environment.

Points Worth Remembering

- Realize that a positive learning culture is key. Build culture first, and learning will follow.
- Develop the culture and then build the structure. Ensure teacher actions are moving students toward end goals.
- Recall the five factors Reeves (2003) identifies that typify the culture in successful 90/90/90 schools.
  a. A focus on academic achievement
  b. Clear curriculum choices
  c. Frequent assessment of student progress and multiple opportunities for improvement
  d. A emphasis on nonfiction writing
  e. Collaborative scoring of student work

- Understand that connected students are successful students. Therefore:
    - Develop positive teacher-student relations, which is one of the most effective steps educators can take to establish a positive learning community
    - Implement structures to minimize the effects of teacher absences
    - Build resilience to increase chances of best student outcomes
    - Teach and form relationships with current students, regardless of their challenges

CLASSROOM EXPECTATIONS

Key 1: Classroom Expectations

Students co-create and condense classroom expectations and codes of conduct into a few easy-to-remember, positively stated words or phrases. Students know the expectations and the adults model them. Behavior expectations link to academic expectations, setting a positive tone. Everyone in the class uses a common language.

Every year, each classroom must establish expectations, routines, predictable structures, and first steps toward creating a learning community where *all* students become proficient in the desired outcomes (behavior and academics). The goal is to create autonomous learners—students who do not require constant adult control and direct supervision and who function both independently and interdependently in the classroom. While it is preferable to do this at the beginning of the school year, teachers reading this should not believe that all hope is lost if the school year is already in progress. It is possible to alter the course and implement expectations later in the school year, provided teachers are prepared to do some additional work.

The first days of class must provide clarity on the positive learning environment the teacher seeks in order to maximize students' experiences. There is a balance between reviewing expectations and beginning with a list of things students cannot do. No students ever went home after the first day of school and relayed to their parents the awesome day they had after being told all the rules and consequences! It is difficult to manage a classroom without consistency and routine, yet it takes experience to establish what works best. Think about the student's learning experiences. What works and what doesn't? Consider the strategy provided at the end of this chapter (page 33). Teachers should think about how best to end the first day and what message each student should take home. New teachers should talk to colleagues for ideas. As teachers determine strategies for managing their classrooms, they should practice them early on and use them consistently. Even the best-behaved students will need to review and practice the expectations and learn some new routines.

When setting expectations for students, teachers should dispel the notion that when students come to the classroom, they can and should leave all of their personal and real-life issues at the door and focus solely on academics. This is not possible, but that should not derail the teacher's intentions. Teachers cannot change the home each student goes to, but they can provide each student with good skills and close the learning gaps as they see students daily, weekly, and monthly during the school year. That is the time for teachers to shine and grow. The expectations teachers hold for students go beyond the four walls of any classroom in any school—they are expectations that will be foundational to students leading healthy and happy lives once their school years are behind them.

Defining Expectations Versus Rules

Key 1 is labeled "Classroom Expectations," and there is a clear intent for this. First, I should make a clear distinction between what I call classroom expectations and traditional classroom rules. *Expectations* serve as guidelines that are important not only in the classroom but, more often than not, also in life beyond the classroom's four walls. Expectations guide student responses academically and behaviorally. Expectations have an emphasis on lifelong learning and an eye toward growth. *Rules*, on the other hand, tend to be specific and are often responses to previous negative outcomes. Rules are attempts to guide student responses, but tend to be reactionary and often do not bring about the desired change.

Classroom rules, often created by adults, appear in the same format year after year. They appear as either preemptive strikes or dire reminders and can be subject to misinterpretation. Classroom expectations, on the other hand, are a few easy-to-remember, positively stated words or phrases co-created with students. This will lead to expectations driven by students, for students. Behavior expectations linked to academic expectations set a positive tone. Everyone in the class should subsequently use a common language when writing and discussing classroom expectations. A common language is essential because individual educators can differ widely in their personal interpretations of typical terms or expectations. For example, I recently asked a group of educators table by table to give me a quick definition of the word *summarize*. I heard responses like *condense*, *rephrase*, *key points*, *main idea*, *shorter version*, and *use your own words*. While I would not dispute the validity of any of these answers, there was enough difference that the group could see how individual interpretations could be problematic and possibly impact students depending on what classroom they ended up in. A common language, established in collaborative time, helps educators develop and maintain expectations that can be universally embraced and understood. When expectations are set up this way, all students will understand them and why they are in place.

The teacher must take care to always model the classroom expectations. Modeling expectations established for others is a challenge and becomes even more so when emotions are part of the response (imagine a teacher *yelling* at students to use their "inside voices"). The only way to ensure the expectations are fully understood and ingrained is by adhering to them in the moment when a student is least able to model them—even when the student's behavior leads to anger and frustration on the part of the teacher. When students are being disrespectful, they will not learn about the importance of respect by an adult out-disrespecting them. This is the time when teachers must set aside emotion and let their passion for student learning drive their response.

Case Study: The Problem With Rules

I once worked with a teacher who had created ten classroom rules with her grade 3 students. She and the students had talked about each one and ultimately created a great poster with each rule written in block letters in a different color. The challenge in this classroom involved a substitute teacher who had not been part of constructing the rules. Students became animated after morning recess, culminating in a mock sword fight with cardboard rolls. This was not covered in the list of ten, so the substitute teacher decided to quickly add rule number eleven (hastily scribbled at the bottom of the poster in purple marker), which read, "No making weapons out of cardboard."

Is there a problem with this addition? For the student who is often on the edge of compliance there are potential problems. What is going through his or her mind at that moment? Is he or she thinking of ways around this new rule by using other materials to make weapons? Is he or she pondering what defines a weapon? The old adage, "Rules are made to be broken," seems appropriate here.

Imagine, instead, that there are three expectations in that same classroom: (1) respect, (2) responsibility, and (3) safety. The dialogue between teacher and student focuses on these items. For example, the teacher could begin a dialogue by saying, "Class, let's talk about what respect looks like during sharing time." Once discussed, managing expectations is possible, even with overt examples like the one about the substitute teacher adding rule number eleven. Rather than creating a new rule, the conversation would turn to being respectful of the classroom as a learning environment. There is much less wiggle room for personalized interpretation. The teacher should model this expectation of respect in all interactions. As an added bonus, respect is a desirable attribute across grade levels, the school, and beyond.

Aligning Beliefs With Practice

When setting classroom expectations, it's important that every classroom teacher does a personal inventory check regarding his or her belief system. A belief system is the guiding principles teachers hold to be true that serve as a lens through which they process and understand new experiences. Often this belief system may originate in a teacher's personal experiences as a student. It may also be influenced by other personal experiences such as family traditions and values, social encounters, community participation, societal cultural values, teacher preparation, professional development, and books or journals a teacher may read. A teacher's belief system is deeply personal and often highly influential over the culture and expectations of the classroom.

Some of the questions teachers should ask themselves include, What are the key aspects of my belief system and how will they come out in my classroom? Am I operating with a view toward a growth mindset or a fixed mindset for all students? Carol Dweck (2006) defines a *fixed mindset* as a perception of intelligence as fixed from birth. Teachers with a *growth mindset* about student intelligence have learning goals for their students because they believe intelligence can be enhanced and developed over time. This growth mindset is vital to increasing success, especially for individuals at risk who might have solidified their belief that school success is not attainable. Teachers must ensure that the expectations they hold for all students drive the potential for growth and improvement, rather than cling to the fixed mindset approach that intelligence is predetermined. The current conditions students face—including intelligence—do not determine outcomes, they just determine the starting points. Teachers overtly and covertly help students plot the course.

The belief system of a teacher plays a significant role in identifying expectations as the beliefs guide practice and priorities, help to determine what is ignored, influence decision making, and shape the relationships in the classroom by delineating valuable types of interactions. Several studies underline the importance of teacher expectations for student learning. Education researcher and professor John Hattie (2009) suggests, "Students are more likely to meet expectations than not, whether or not those expectations are good, bad, correct, or misguided" (p. 122). A 1999 study by researchers Karen and Karl Schilling notes that expectations of students' abilities to succeed are vital to their education: "The literature on motivation and school performance in younger school children suggests that expectations shape the learning experience very powerfully" (p. 5). Hattie (2009) validates this concept when he suggests that the question around expectations and success is not, "Do teachers have expectations?" but rather, "Do they have false and misleading expectations that lead to decrements in learning or learning gains . . .?" (p. 121). A further study by Monica J. Harris and Robert Rosenthal (1985) investigating the effects of teachers' expectations on behavioral outcomes confirms a "self-fulfilling prophecy," when teachers are "more likely to have their students reach their 'expected' outcomes, regardless of the veracity of the expectations" (as cited in Hattie, 2009, p. 122). In sum, research has shown that the teacher's mindset and expectations for students play a substantial role in how those students will ultimately perform; as a result, student outcomes will likely improve if teachers approach their expectations from a mindset of growth.

Belief systems of the students themselves—which can be self-developed or influenced by the teacher—can also affect student outcomes. Researchers Lisa S. Blackwell, Kali H. Trzesniewski, and Carol Dweck (2007) followed 373 students making the transition to seventh grade. At the start of that school year they assessed the mindsets of each student (fixed or growth) and then monitored the students' mathematics grades over the next two years. It is important to note that students with fixed and growth mindsets had entered the seventh grade with equal prior mathematics achievement. In as little as one semester, the mathematics grades of the two groups had separated, and they continued to diverge over the next two years. In analyzing the divergence, the authors suggest that three key variables emerged that highlight the difference between students with a growth mindset versus those with a fixed mindset.

1. Students with the growth mindset were significantly more oriented toward learning goals. Although they cared about their grades, they cared even more about learning.

2. Students with the growth mindset showed a far stronger belief in the power of effort. They believed that effort promoted ability and that effort was effective regardless of their current level of ability.

3. Students with the growth mindset showed more mastery-oriented reactions to setbacks, being less likely to denigrate their ability and more likely to employ positive strategies, such as greater effort and new strategies, rather than negative strategies, such as effort withdrawal and cheating.

In the final analysis, the authors suggest that students who have a fixed mindset but who are well prepared and do not encounter difficulties will learn and perform material just fine. The divergence in achievement occurs, however, when these students encounter challenges or obstacles that put them at a disadvantage. At this point, the differences in mindset appear to strongly affect academic outcomes.

On many levels, the success of classroom expectations rests on the classroom culture. (Refer to chapter 1 on page 7 for more on classroom culture.) A growth mindset is indicative of a healthy culture where the teacher strives to create policies, practices, and procedures that align with the belief of growth being the outcome for *all* students (Cromwell, 2002). A fixed mindset, on the other hand, aligns with what Kent Peterson describes as a toxic culture predicated on the belief that "student success is based solely upon a student's level of concern, attentiveness, prior knowledge, and the willingness to comply with the demands of school" (Cromwell, 2002). Teachers will inevitably create policies, procedures, and practices that further their beliefs, whatever they are.

Setting Up Your Classroom

In *Pyramid of Behavior Interventions*, the authors stress the importance of each classroom's expectations aligning with the school's overarching expectations (Hierck et al., 2011). While that still holds true, it is equally important that individual teachers also establish unique expectations and priorities within their own classrooms. These should be complementary, not competing, expectations.

There are differences in both the nature of some classroom spaces (for example, the gymnasium versus a typical subject-area classroom) and the classroom content (woodworking versus music or mathematics), and teachers must consider these differences when setting up their unique learning environments for success. Likewise, each teacher displays a different personal style when instructing, and this individual autonomy needs to be considered not in terms of what expectations are being delivered, but how. No matter how the expectations are taught, one factor is key: classroom expectations must always be designed with the students in mind. Bill Krefft, a grade 8 special education teacher, talks about this important aspect in his classroom:

> It is critically important when setting up classroom systems to understand that chasing excellence is everything. So often, I find that classroom teachers apply the terms "student centered" and "data driven" to their instructional strategies but not to their classroom routines and procedures. It is more important to have the culture of your classroom be student centered and data driven than any other aspect. If you build all of your routines and systems based on student need, everything else will happen naturally. (personal communication, June 2, 2014)

The key component to setting classroom expectations is to begin immediately. Although I am abundantly aware of the time demands on teachers, I also know that teachers spend a great deal of non-school time on their craft. If possible, some of this time should be allotted to classroom setup, which includes planning classroom expectations in addition to physically preparing the classroom. A critical time for classroom setup to occur is at the start of the school year. Spend some additional time setting up the classroom to make it an inviting learning space. Provide stimulating, educational distractions on the walls. Connect these to your bigger goals (respect, responsibility, safety, growth mindset, to name a few) and have them serve as focal points for students. If the classroom setup does not occur early in the school year, when students are looking for structure and cues about what conduct is acceptable, establishing expectations will become a constant struggle throughout the school year.

Failing to set up classroom expectations early results in what I identify as *chase time*. Loosely defined, chase time is the time lost from teaching or other proactive activities that is instead spent trying to retroactively set expectations after bad habits have already been set. Chase time generally occurs reactively and is an adult's attempt to reteach a lesson after a student demonstrates that he or she is deficient in some particular skill. It is the proverbial closing-the-barn-door-after-the-horses-have-left response and rarely produces the kinds of positive learning environments necessary in classrooms. While chase time is unavoidable in certain situations, educators can minimize it by making expectations clear from the very first day of school so that students begin the year practicing desired behaviors, not bad ones.

Establishing Classroom Expectations With Students

As I mentioned in the opening to this chapter, it is important that classroom expectations are created with students. This helps to develop a sense of ownership in creating a positive learning environment. Students at any age have powerful insights into what should and what should not occur in a class where learning is the prime objective. Framing these insights as expectations avoids the rush to establish consequences that often accompanies the process of rule creation. Alignment with the overarching school expectations is a desired outcome and may help in shaping some of the parameters for student contributions.

As part of establishing classroom expectations, teachers may have to temper some of the suggestions students offer when there is noncompliance for the desired expectations. I have sat in on many conversations where students offered quite severe consequences for failing to meet basic expectations. My reminder to them (and to teachers) is that a classroom is a teaching and learning space first. Failure to meet the desired expectations may represent a behavioral skill gap that is very similar to an academic skill gap, and teachers should use an instructional approach as part of the remediation, instead of rushing to harsh consequences. (How to set appropriate consequences for when expectations [not rules] are violated will be defined and discussed on page 47 in the Direct to Correct to Connect section.)

Equally important in ensuring that conversations around student expectations have meaning and value is teacher modeling. The students' eyes are always on the teacher. If the teacher doesn't model what he or she teaches, then the teacher is teaching what he or she models. This may or may not align with the classroom or school expectations.

One personal example of this was borne out of some negative practice I engaged in early in my career. Despite having *respect* as one of my foundational expectations, I still raised my voice and devalued students in front of their peers when I was disciplining them. I was not delivering on the promise of a respectful learning environment. I can recall with great clarity when this turned around and the profound, positive impact it had on my class. The day after losing my temper with some students, I faced the same group again. I had a choice to make, and my choice was between two options.

1. Remind the students of my blast from the previous day and let them know that today I was even closer to the edge. I could give it my best Clint Eastwood impersonation and ask the previous day's perpetrator if he felt lucky.

2. Remind the class of the expectation of respect and issue a complete apology for my lack of adherence to this expectation. Not to excuse any behavior on the part of a student that was disrespectful, but to do my part in showing what respect looks like, even in a challenging situation.

As you can probably surmise, I chose the second option. I'm not sure if this was a courageous action on my part or simply the realization that something had to change. It was fascinating to watch the turnaround in class. Students took on greater responsibility for both their own personal accountability and that of the larger group. They reminded each other of the expectation of respect and took ownership of it. I still had the occasional incident where a student was noncompliant, but I processed it from the perspective of respect and that made all the difference. Teachers should make this same commitment when setting classroom expectations: always aim to model the classroom expectations, but if (or when) a slip occurs, apologize, take accountability for the error, and recommit to the classroom expectations.

Establishing Routines

From the moment they arrive in the classroom, students should know the teacher's expectations. This can be achieved by the teacher immediately establishing daily tasks and routines that clarify for the students how the day will be run. Does the teacher start class with a problem of the day that students can begin to address the moment they enter or will students receive it three minutes into the start of class? Or is the start of class a little unstructured with last-minute preparation, attendance checks, retrieving copies left in the office, and general chaos that changes from day to day (or even period to period)? Students crave structure and organization (Battistich & Hom, 1997; Hawkins, Catalano, Kosterman, Abbott,

& Hill, 1999; Resnick et al., 1997), and teachers can assist in this by providing predictable daily routines.

If the start of class is seemingly unimportant, is it surprising that many teachers must deal with tardy students? I learned this lesson the hard way when I transitioned from being a full-time teacher to a vice principal with a teaching component. I failed to build in a routine that took into account the other responsibilities I had assumed with my new assignment. Often I would get to class harried and unprepared with little beginning structure to ignite learning in my students—and they knew it! I began to notice that on-time arrival to my class became arrival *just before the teacher arrives*. My entrance to the room meant dealing with a series of demands, an attempt to check who was there, a lament about their tardiness, and a lack of routine. I initially put the responsibility of my students' lack of engagement on them. It was only during a class meeting (an excellent strategy I'll talk more about later in this chapter beginning on page 31), when I posed the question about their lethargy and lack of success toward the subject, that the reality emerged. From the back of the room came a clear, loud (and, I know now, exceedingly accurate) request, "Have you considered not being boring?"

I have to admit—that comment stung, but it hit the mark. The student was communicating that my class had failed to engage him at the start of each period. My scrambling approach to beginning a lesson meant the hook to the learning was missing and I was missing a structured approach to engaging them, instead "winging it" each day and relying on my knowledge of the content. The lack of routine to start the class meant students would often fail to initiate any inquiry. By simply building in routines such as the problem of the day (POD, which I could put on the board the day before), student self–sign in, and having them place requested work in their portfolios, the students' attitudes shifted to become more positive. We also developed a classroom arrival routine: my arrival now signaled group time consisting of me delivering content, probing responses to previous work, or structuring groups for the day's activities. Though this attitude shift was promising and affected student outcomes positively, it took more time than it would have had I begun the year off right and anticipated some of the challenges my new responsibilities would create. I was reminded of the importance of beginning the school year with routines that complement my classroom values and expectations.

Kelly Holmes, a grade 1 teacher, also understands the importance of starting the year off right:

Routines and procedures are what make things work in my classroom. We begin those the moment they enter our room. Kids have to physically do something repeatedly before it becomes routine to them. Why not start the first days of school? I always try to use every moment I have with them to teach them how things will work in our classroom because I've found that more learning will take place if these things are set up immediately. (Personal communication, June 24, 2014)

Routines assist teachers as much as they assist students. Knowing what a good lesson looks like and striving to achieve that goal ensures the desired outcome. Redundancy builds fluency—the more we practice routines, the better we get at them and the more successful they are when implemented.

Over the years a number of practices have produced high levels of success. The following examples are offered as suggestions to help teachers establish routines, but are not required in every classroom. It is critically important that teachers consider the individual contexts of their communities, their schools, and their students when modifying these practices to best suit their needs. As mentioned above, routines need to become fully integrated into the expectations of a successful classroom experience. These routines may be organizational, such as group arrangement or class meetings, or they may be functional, such as assignment turn-in. Regardless, it's the practice of routines and the acknowledgment of growing proficiency that will add to the positive learning environment you're striving to create.

Arranging Groups

One valuable routine to establish in your classroom is exposing students to regular group work. The value of collaborative work time can become even more beneficial if there is a strong emphasis on collaboration skills and if the groups change frequently, giving participants the opportunity to work with a diverse group of people. The task of sorting students into groups, often done by the students themselves, can seem like a chore. Affiliation or expectation of a certain academic level often dictate their selections. This tends to lead to the establishment of very familiar groups and undermines the potential growth that could occur when students are grouped randomly with the objective of learning to authentically collaborate. However, sorting students into groups does not need to be a tedious task. It can be a fun activity and even include some academic content. Some ideas for sorting students into work groups include the following.

◆ Randomly hand out cards with various images such as bacon, eggs, and sausages; strawberries, blueberries, and blackberries; and other groups of things (one on each card). Then ask students to find someone with a card that complements their card.

◆ Take a pack of playing cards and randomly distribute the kings, queens, jacks, and so on. Students then form teams accordingly. For example, a group could compriseall red jacks or all the royal court in a single suit.

◆ Prepare a bag of clean socks. Each student picks one then finds its mate. For larger groups, pairs join other pairs by size or color.

This activity can also have an academic focus to it by adding some current content.

◆ Students create four cards that each feature a fun fact about a state or province. These cards then become the foundation for the group-selection process (that is, all holders of the four fact cards about the same state or province form one group).

◆ Students develop cards with addition, subtraction, multiplication, and division problems. For each card with a mathematics problem, there is another card with the answer. Students solve the problem to determine their partner.

◆ Teachers place cards, each with a Spanish (or any other language) word, face down on a table or stack. Students pick a card, find their partner with the same word in the different language, talk about the word (making a sentence, sharing a story, and so on), and then continue working as partners for the lesson.

Turning in Assignments

Assignment turn-in is another area that can cause great consternation and frustration for teachers. Getting students to turn in their completed work reminds some of raking leaves in a high wind—lots of effort, but little accumulation. When establishing a classroom routine for assignment turn-in, reflect on previously used strategies and ask the reflective question, How did they work? If the strategy worked well, keep doing it! If not, and the consequences imposed did not change the outcome, try something else. Some of the assignment turn-in routines I have found to be most successful, particularly when used to supplement classroom expectations, are listed in the following paragraph.

One of the most effective approaches to assignment collection is the use of a student folder, binder, or portfolio. All students have a folder, binder, or portfolio in which they place their work. Teachers should work with students to set agreed-on requirements for the number and type of work samples to include. Teachers should consider the time, inclination, and need to see everything students complete before setting these requirements with student input. Teachers may increase the potential for higher-quality portfolio submissions and higher completion rates for each student if they request a variety of assignments to be turned in—for example, if there is a requirement to submit an example of best work, an example of work that reflects the most learning, samples driven by specific content or subject area, and an example of group work during a fixed period of time. Eighth-grade special education teacher Bill Krefft talks about using student folders and the positive outcomes realized from the practice:

> *I like the idea of having individual student folders that are kept in the classroom so students take ownership for their materials. These folders allow me to individualize accommodations based on need without drawing attention from other students because everyone has their own folder. These individual folders allow students to manage their progress and growth easier as they always have their "To Do, Already Done" list at their immediate disposal. This allows the students to visualize their progress on a daily basis, not based on grade, but based on growth. (Personal communication, June 2, 2014)*

Meeting as a Class

Teachers can use class meetings as an effective, multipurpose tool. This proactive strategy sets aside time for students to discuss classroom issues as a group. Class meetings can yield significant benefits, such as helping to set the tone for respectful learning, establishing a climate of trust, developing empathy, and encouraging collaboration. While each teacher and class needs to contextualize this approach so that it works best, it is beneficial to hold this meeting at a regular weekly time. As little as twenty to thirty minutes, if the meeting is well organized, should suffice.

The purpose behind this strategy is to get students involved in constructive decision making in their classrooms. It also builds a climate of trust and respect between the teacher and students and between students. Given a chance to make meaningful and purposeful contributions, students' senses of responsibility and efficacy will increase. They will take greater ownership of problems *and* solutions.

Holding regular classroom meetings allows teachers to create classrooms in which students feel comfortable to learn, safe to share their ideas, and free to ask questions and take risks. In addition to forming a dependable routine for students, this technique also helps build relationships among students and between students and the teacher. (Please see chapter 1 for more information on the importance of teacher-student relationship building.)

A possible design for classroom meetings could include the following steps.

- Meetings are held weekly.
- Meetings follow a set format.
- Students sit on chairs in a circle.
- Students lead the meetings.
- Teacher(s) and students discuss both problems and solutions.
- Students encourage and compliment one another.

In order to incorporate class meetings and have them be a positive activity, teachers must prepare students during the first weeks of school. The teacher should structure lessons to teach and help students practice the key skills needed for positive class meetings, such as encouragement, creative problem solving, and circle formation. The teacher should lead the first few meetings and model the process. In short order, students should take over as meeting leaders, with each student taking a turn as discussion leader during the school year. As with any group dynamic, there is the potential for emotion to take over and for class meetings to digress into "name, shame, and blame" gatherings. This is when the importance of group norms comes into play and when the teacher may need to remind students of the agreed-on norms as they develop their skills. Ultimately students will need to own the norms and remind each other when a violation occurs.

Working With Students who Challenge Us

In my long career as an educator, this truism has emerged: students who challenge teachers the most need teachers the most. These students may not be able or willing to admit it, but they often display behaviors and attitudes that would convince most adults that they do not want teachers intervening in their lives or supporting them on the road to success. Teachers must look beyond the façade and bravado to discover what underpins this behavior. Saving face is often more important to these students than admitting they are struggling. It seems much more cool for a student to call out ,"Math sucks!" than to admit that he or she is deficient in the basics of mathematics and, therefore, can't complete the work today.

One strategy teachers can use when working with challenging students is to put aside any preconceived notions of that student. Many times when teachers begin the school year, they receive word about a particular "problem" student who will be in their class. This hearsay may have even occurred the previous year, resulting in a tension-fraught summer filled with concern about how the child will behave in the coming school year. Imagine that, instead of focusing on hearsay from colleagues and predetermining how to enact discipline at the first sign of trouble, teachers embark on a plan to be the difference maker in this particular child's life. Imagine what could occur if teachers decide instead to make this year the problem child's best year yet. They could set the stage for growth by immediately establishing clear classroom expectations and routines and work to ensure that all students learn and practice the expectations, regardless of their history. With these structures in place, all students will be primed to have a better year and learn more. Additionally, the teachers will hand off a student who is further along than the one they inherited at the beginning of the year. This is, in essence, what the teacher's role needs to be: committing to every student growing under his or her watch.

A Strategy to Consider

Teachers should end the first day of school with clarity around what the year will hold in order to create a sense of hope for all students. Let each student know that he or she will be writing a book, and that each day will produce a new page. The teacher should also ask students what they want their personal 180-page books (or number of school days) to convey. Promise the students inspiring teaching in exchange for their promise of inspiring reads.

Points Worth Remembering

- The best time to set expectations is at the beginning of the year, but anytime is better than not at all.
- Expectations are often preferable to rules. They should be co-created with students and condensed into a few easy-to-remember, positively stated words or phrases.

- Expectations should align with teacher beliefs.
- Teachers should nurture a mindset of growth for all students.
- All staff should model expectations regularly.
- Routines provide consistency for students and can supplement classroom expectations.
    - Use activities to divide students into groups that then work collaboratively to complete the lesson.
    - Establish routines for turning in assignments and following up when items are late.
    - Hold regular class meetings and teach students effective use, practice, and norms to make these an effective tool.
- The students who challenge teachers the most often need teachers the most.

TARGETED
INSTRUCTION

Key 2: Targeted Instruction

All staff directly teach classroom expectations to students in a myriad of ways and in various specific settings (in class, in the library, during assemblies, on the bus, and so on). Students receive opportunities to develop, practice, and demonstrate appropriate social and academic skills. Students learn social skills in the same manner as academic skills: demonstrate, practice, review, and celebrate.

It is imperative that students feel comfortable in their learning community because without feelings of safety and comfort, they will never be able to take in quality instruction. Much is made of the importance of using Bloom's taxonomy to structure challenging work for students that will build their capacity as learners. What sometimes gets lost during instruction is the importance of Maslow's hierarchy of needs. The lower two levels of Maslow's hierarchy are defined as basic needs and they become increasingly motivating the longer they are unmet. If students show up to school hungry or tired, they may be more fixated on those needs than on the day's lesson. If this pattern is repeated and students' basic needs are continually unmet, the chances of academic uptake severely decrease. Thus, these basic needs teachers must provide before a student can progress and meet higher-level growth needs. Similarly, the lower levels of Bloom's taxonomy focus on the lowest level of cognition (thinking), which requires students to recall information in basically the same form it was presented or take several bits of information and put them into a single category or grouping. Students must master these entry points before they can achieve higher-level thinking skills. Simply put, you cannot effectively implement the Bloom stuff if you haven't taken care of the Maslow stuff. (See figure 3.1.)

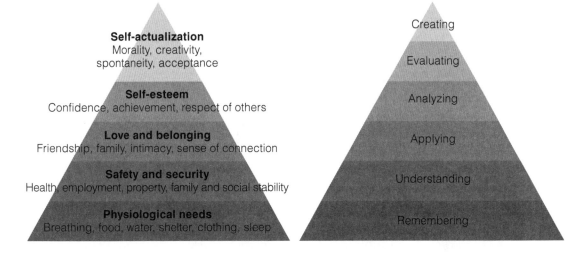

Figure 3.1: Maslow's hierarchy of needs and Bloom's taxonomy.

*Visit **go.SolutionTree.com/behavior** for a free reproducible version of this figure.*

The premise of targeted instruction is for a teacher to identify the expectations and the strategies that he or she believes will have the greatest impact on student learning outcomes. Before that can be attained, the teacher must first establish a positive learning environment that helps meet all students' basic needs. For students who did not get to eat before school, some teachers I have met choose to keep a stash of quick and easy snacks on hand. For students who lack a sense of love and belonging, teachers can establish this feeling in the classroom by opening themselves up to the class and sharing some of who they are. The "Bag of Me" is a great strategy to facilitate this. The teacher will get a large bag and place ten items from his or her life inside. Individual students will pull out an item and the teacher then provides the story behind the item. Students then get to know their teacher on a more personal level and realize everybody has a story beyond what can be seen on the surface. Once this caring and understanding environment has been set up, teachers can move on to teaching the expectations and targeting instruction to fit the context of their classrooms.

Teaching Expectations

In the previous chapter we talked about the need to establish classroom expectations, not rules. Once established, the next critical step is to teach those expectations. Remember that students will not become fluent in these expectations in the absence of clear instruction. We wouldn't expect that to occur with academic expectations, so it makes little sense to expect fluency to occur in the behavioral domain without explicit instruction. Early in the school year is the best time to teach expectations and then provide opportunities for students to develop them. Without this early instruction, it is likely that you will continue to wrestle with the same challenges in month seven of the school year as you did in month one. Practicing the expectations so they become daily routines will lead to the desired outcomes early in the school year.

Some students' behavior affects and impedes their learning and potentially the learning of others. As a result, teachers must start with teaching the desired or expected behaviors. Let's look at the expectation of respect. How might this look in terms of desired behaviors? An example might be that students show respect for their classroom by pushing in their chairs when they are not working at their desks or when they leave the room. This seems like a simple task, and it may seem like students should already know how to do this. However, if it's not occurring to your expected level, it's an indicator that this principle has not been taught the way that works best for you. So, teach it! Review the expectations, model them, give students an opportunity to practice, and reinforce or remediate the desired behaviors when they are or are not occurring. It is important to remember that even when students have been involved in the creation of the expectations, they still need to be held to a standard. This standard only becomes reasonable when students have been taught how to reach it and given opportunities to demonstrate and practice the standard. Staff must teach and give such opportunities to students in a variety of ways.

The teacher doesn't have to be a behavior specialist to convey his or her expectations to students and teach them effectively. He or she simply has to know ahead of time what behaviors are desirable and be able to model them. Additionally, it's vitally important to teach classroom expectations in context. For example, can a teacher teach a student about appropriate restroom behavior in the classroom? The answer, of course, is no, as a school restroom does not resemble a classroom. The expectation of appropriate restroom behavior (using the toilet correctly, washing and drying hands, and putting garbage in the garbage can) must be practiced in that location. It is also important to consider the differing contexts that occur in different areas of the school. A gymnasium has different factors to consider (size, noise level, shared space) than a regular classroom might have.

A high school might have a designated smoking area or an elementary school might have a forested area by the playground. All of these unique contexts would demand further clarifications of the expectations and an opportunity to practice those expectations in those contexts.

When preparing to teach behavioral expectations in the classroom, teachers must recognize that appropriate behavior takes time for students to learn and implement. In 2009, researchers at the University College of London asked the question, "How long does it take to form a habit?" (Lally, van Jaarsveld, Potts, & Wardle, 2010, p. 998). The results suggest that it can take anywhere from 18 to 254 days, but 66 days represents a sweet spot, with easier behaviors taking fewer days and tough ones taking more days. Teachers should keep this in mind as they think about their first steps in teaching the desired expectations!

Case Study: The Importance of Teaching Behavioral Skills

Imagine a student, Billy, is struggling in mathematics with division problems that focus on dividing three-digit numbers by two-digit numbers. The teacher notices his struggle and tells Billy that he has one more chance to demonstrate his ability to solve the problem. Clearly, Billy is no further ahead in his capacity to solve the problem and continues to struggle. The teacher comes by again and tells Billy he has run out of chances and will now need to receive a consequence.

To many, this outcome will seem preposterous. Billy may need to be taught (or retaught) strategies to solve this problem before he can be expected to demonstrate a different outcome. Some teachers might see this as a typical Tier 2 problem needing an intervention of some type to close the gap. Some might even suggest monitoring Billy's progress to see if the intervention is having the desired effect. Early screening may reveal that Billy is struggling with Tier 3 basic, foundational skills, and he may need immediate, intensive support to close this gap while the gap is manageable. However, if the same scenario included a behavior challenge, like talking out during instruction, many of those same objecting voices would be mute, and others would suggest the outcome was reasonable. They might assume that Billy is simply engaging in "won't do" behavior that is vastly different from "can't do" academic struggles.

Far too often, teachers see behavior struggles as different challenges than academic struggles. They treat behavioral situations in terms of outcomes and punishment. However, just as there are academic gaps, there are gaps in desired behaviors like self-regulation, executive functioning, and organization skills. Teachers should use the same instructional design and process for inextricably linked behavior and academics. Where should a teacher begin? Hattie (2012) offers some great insight when he suggests, "Attention needs to move from how to teach to how to learn—and only after teachers understand how each student learns can they then move on to make decisions about how to teach" (p. 92).

Reviewing Expectations

Teachers should demonstrate, practice, review, and then celebrate the desired expectations when students model them. When students fail to perform desired behaviors as expected, the questions a teacher should ask are these: Were the students ever taught the desired behavior? Did the teacher model it? Did students practice the desired behavior? Was their practice reviewed for correctness? And was a positive demonstration reinforced? In essence, did the teacher show the students how to properly raise their hands (all five fingers up, no pumping of the arm or audible sounds, no waving) and provide a moment to have each child demonstrate? Were early miscues viewed as opportunities to reteach and were successful demonstrations celebrated? This becomes the structure for teachers to reintroduce expectations and facilitate their development in students. (The topic of how positive reinforcement is an absolute necessity for teachers in establishing a positive learning environment will be further discussed in chapter 4, page 45.)

Teachers and students should work together to set appropriate consequences for when expectations are not modeled. Let's go back to Billy (see the case study on page 38) and imagine that his behavioral challenges come from a lack of attentiveness. What might constitute an instructional approach that teachers could take before rushing to punitive consequences? Table 3.1 (page 40) lists some possible causes of inattentiveness and provides suggestions for proactively addressing the cause.

Table 3.1: Causes and Solutions for Inattentiveness

Cause	Possible Remedy
Schedule	Provide students with a visible, tangible schedule of the lesson or day's activities. Teachers must be organized and follow the schedule at a brisk pace, with minimal lost time for transitions.
Clutter	Remove any items students do not need for current tasks. Distractible students behave better when their work area is uncluttered.
Tasks	Save easier tasks for later in the lesson or the end of the day as this is typically when attention wanes. Avoid long stretches of instructional time in which students sit passively.
Focus	Capture students' attention through predictable structures, routines, and procedures. Wait until all students are present before giving directions. Use a strategy that works for you (for example, "One, two, eyes on you. One, two, three, eyes on me"). Privately approach targeted students to restate directions or have the students restate them.
Breaks	Agree to give students short breaks to engage in a preferred activity when they have finished a given amount of work.

*Visit **go.SolutionTree.com/behavior** for a free reproducible version of this table.*

Let's pick a strategy from table 3.1 that we could apply to Billy and his penchant for calling out at inappropriate times. Perhaps Billy's teacher may choose "Focus," trying to capture Billy's attention through a predictable routine. The teacher would wait until Billy was attentive before giving directions. He or she might privately approach Billy to provide directions and have him restate them. The teacher would also work with Billy to establish appropriate consequences for what should happen if Billy fails to meet expectations. Billy's correct demonstration of the desired behaviors would then result in a form of acknowledgment targeted to Billy's need (from extrinsic to intrinsic) as he continues on his path to behavioral proficiency.

Please note that table 3.1 represents a next step in the teaching cycle and assumes that all students know the desired expectations as part of the teacher's universal instruction. It's important to keep in mind that the more challenging the behavioral deficit, the more unique the response needs to be. While the strategies presented in table 3.1 will work for the majority of our students, there are occasions when a student will demonstrate a behavior that a teacher may not yet have encountered. At this time, teachers may choose a collaborative approach to invite colleagues to suggest another strategy or alternatively search their own toolboxes to reveal a response or technique not routinely used but potentially highly effective. Remember that responses to challenging behavior may need to be tailored to students' unique needs.

Tailoring Teaching: DNA and Building Relationships

All students arrive to school with their own dreams, needs, and abilities (or desires, needs, and assets—DNA). Cassandra Erkens (2016) introduced this later version of DNA and suggests, "When teachers and learners work together, they can isolate the individual's *learning DNA*. . . . Such data are invaluable in the teaching and learning process" (p. 156). The more teachers can tap into what motivates students and what students bring to the classroom each day, the more they can target instruction to those needs. Learning this at the beginning of every school year and adjusting to each student's unique information as students grow during the year will set up every teacher for the opportunity to successfully plan for each student. This is an excellent way for teachers to achieve the basic levels of Maslow's hierarchy and build a sense of community.

One of the most effective ways I've seen teachers tailor their teaching to students' unique DNA is through the work of Woodridge, Illinois, Assistant Superintendent Greg Wolcott and the educators at the district's seven schools. They call their approach "Significant 72," which involves taking the first three days of school and strictly devoting this time to building effective relationships. You can find more information on the Significant 72 in *Starting a Movement* (Williams & Hierck, 2015). This work is based on the notion of having teachers know their students individually, having the students know them, and having the students know each other. Once the teachers have established relationships with the students individually and know how best to teach and respond to each one of them, their teaching will substantially improve. John Hattie and Gregory Yates (2014) say of the impact of teacher-student relationships:

> *The positive teacher-student relationship is thus important not so much because this is worthwhile in itself, but because it helps build the trust to make mistakes, to ask for help, to build confidence to try again, and for students to know they will not look silly when they don't get it the first time. (p. 21)*

Targeted teaching based on students' individual needs can be especially beneficial for *at-risk students*—those students who have a higher probability of failing
academically or dropping out of school. These students may require temporary or
ongoing intervention in order to succeed academically. In particular, "at-risk students (lower SES/learning difficulties) benefited more from strong relationships
with teachers" (Roorda, Koomen, Spilt, & Oort, 2011, p. 518).

I often hear that targeting teaching by establishing a relationship with each student individually becomes more challenging as students move into the secondary
school environment because of timetable issues (more teachers or classrooms)
and the focus shift to academic content. Sometimes teachers may avoid building
relationships with older students because they feel older students may not need
this, or because they don't believe teacher-student relationships can be important
at that age. However, Roorda et al. (2011) found the opposite effect, stating,
"Positive relationships were particularly beneficial to older students, and overall,
'stronger effects were found in higher grades'" (p. 517). Similarly, Anne Gregory
and Rhona S. Weinstein (2004) found, when investigating academic outcomes
in a population of mathematics students, that "the single most important school-
based predictor of academic growth in mathematics—from the eighth to twelfth
grades—was a student's perception of 'connectedness' with his teachers" (p. 424).
Thus, despite the preconceptions that teachers may initially have about the efficacy of building individual relationships with their students, research indicates
that efforts to develop relationships with students are in fact beneficial to students, regardless of age. It's clear that using the skill of relationship building (that
is, discovering every student's DNA) allows teachers to take the next steps in
designing high-quality instruction for *all* students.

Avoiding Potential Hazards to Targeted Instruction

When targeting instruction to individual students, be careful not to undermine
the teacher-student relationship. To illustrate this, let's consider the example of
a seating plan. Many teachers employ seating plans in targeted teaching to assist
students with special needs (such as poor eyesight or hearing), but a seating plan
can also be a punishment or consequence for bad behavior. When assigned seating becomes the consequence for off-task behaviors, the seat nearest the teacher
can become a negative attribute and work against positive relationships forming

between students and the teacher. This is an example of where the intention of the approach (beneficial versus consequential) for the student could mitigate some of the stigma attached to the approach. A better approach may be communicating to students, in unemotional language, that they are being moved for their benefit (to get more practice in the desired outcomes or as an opportunity to learn organization skills). In this proactive situation, teachers can convey a potential for learning, rather than a negative stigma.

Remember, classrooms are teaching and learning environments first and foremost, and this belief must extend to the desired behavioral outcomes that arise as a result of targeted instruction. If we can predict undesirable behaviors, we can prevent them. Teachers know early on (and often have evidence from previous years) about potential struggles that may arise in their classrooms. Failing to address these anticipated struggles intentionally, and not targeting your instruction to close the gap, is tantamount to condoning the wrong behavior. The best way to achieve the desired behavior for all students is to intentionally teach those desired behaviors.

A Strategy to Consider

The simple "2 by 10 strategy" requires teachers to spend two minutes per day for ten consecutive days talking with an at-risk student about anything he or she wants to talk about. The strategy builds a rapport and relationship between teacher and student and lets the student see that the teacher genuinely cares about him or her as a person. Grade 8 special education teacher Bill Krefft says, "Teacher-student rapport is the single greatest factor that will contribute to the success of both the student and the teacher" (personal communication, June 2, 2014).

Points Worth Remembering

- Students must feel comfortable in their learning environment before they can learn effectively. Focus on Maslow's hierarchy of needs before working on Bloom's taxonomy.
- There is an inextricable link between behavior and academics.
- Teaching expectations and building habits will take time.

- Educators must be intentional in teaching behavioral expectations and prepared to differentiate for students who are not proficient.
- Teachers should demonstrate, practice, review, and then celebrate the desired expectations when students model them.
- Teachers should learn every student's DNA (dreams, needs, and abilities).
- Avoid teaching and disciplining strategies that undermine teacher-student relationships.

POSITIVE REINFORCEMENT

Key 3: Positive Reinforcement

Students receive timely and specific feedback—both formally and informally—on a regular basis. Celebration, recognition, and reward systems are in place to acknowledge, honor, and thank students for displaying positive social and academic skills.

Feedback is the information a teacher provides to a student in terms of that student's understanding or demonstration of learning. It is most often an outcome of learning as opposed to a stimulus for learning. Yet, at its most powerful, feedback has the potential to improve teaching and learning if educators utilize different types of feedback and assess their effectiveness during the teaching-learning cycle. The relationship between assessment and feedback is a critical component of this back-and-forth exchange.

Timely and specific feedback is critical to improved learning. Students crave feedback and regularly seek it out. In a fascinating study, researcher Graham Nuthall (2007) put microphones on students and analyzed what was happening for them each day. One of the more interesting discoveries he made was that 80 percent of the feedback students received each day was from other students—and 80 percent of it was wrong! In discussion with students, Nuthall found out they like receiving the feedback. Why? Because, despite the inaccuracies, the feedback satisfies two key criteria for feedback to be effective: *just in time* and *just for me*. The timeliness aspect makes sense as the shorter the time lag, the smaller the gap, and the easier it is to close. If teachers delay feedback, students lose the opportunity for improvement. In progressive learning, students will not achieve the next step in the process if they have not yet mastered the previous step. I often encounter high school teachers frustrated with students reading at a grade 3 level. But when did teachers first know about the gap, and when could they first have provided feedback to close it? Grade 3, or possibly even earlier. The challenge becomes more significant and more difficult to amend with each passing day, week, or month. Educators should take care to personalize feedback as each student has unique needs. It's rarely an effective strategy to offer the whole class feedback unless the whole class has made the same mistake. In my experience this is a rare occasion!

Teachers should provide feedback both formally and informally on a regular basis. Beyond the grade at the end of an assignment, formal feedback includes strategies like the daily agenda (an outline of the activities and discussions that will occur that day), clear instructions, or review of assignments. Informal feedback includes the minute-by-minute exchanges that occur with students. The formal expectations at the end of a period of learning or grade are positively impacted by the informal feedback teachers provide.

Teachers should implement feedback in the form of celebration, recognition, and reward systems to acknowledge, honor, and thank students for displaying positive social and academic skills. In *Pyramid of Behavior Interventions*, Hierck et al. (2011, pages 49–50) identify a variety of examples of this feedback, and I'd like to add one more to the list. A number of schools I've worked with have embarked on a schoolwide initiative for improving behavior that begins with recognition in the classroom. Moving beyond a classroom celebration, these schools have taken to having a large receptacle outside the main office called the JAR (Just Acting Right). Each time a student exhibits a positive behavior, they receive a token that gets placed in the JAR. When the JAR is full, a schoolwide celebration occurs. I often get asked about this being effective at the secondary grades and my response is always the same. I don't know of any person who does not appreciate authentic, meaningful, and personalized acknowledgment.

Feedback From Teachers to Students

As teachers look to find additional tools to add to their feedback toolbox, it's often helpful to turn to colleagues and hear about some other strategies. As with any tool, it's important to contextualize to ensure what you know about your class and your students is included when implementing the strategy. Here are some examples to consider.

Direct to Correct to Connect

As teachers shift the focus away from negative consequences to positive outcomes, it becomes increasingly important to anchor feedback with a blueprint to guide both teacher and student actions. Imagine a typical classroom where one of the foundational expectations is respect. The teacher has articulated the importance of respect and has modeled it consistently with the class. The teacher even provides examples of what respect looks like for students. For example, the teacher has told students that when one person is talking, everyone else should be listening. If a student has a thought in response to the person talking and he or she would like to share a thought, the respectful thing to do would be to raise his or her hand. Despite these clear behavior guidelines, one student continues to call out and interrupt the class. This is where a teacher must make a clear decision between negative (consequences) and positive (outcomes) through the direct to correct to connect continuum.

In the *direct* approach, the teacher simply tells the student what to do and indicates (or administers) the consequence. The language sounds something like, "Suzie, please raise your hand. I've told you on a number of occasions to do that and the next time I hear you call out will result in a detention!" This threat does little to teach, and it's fairly easy to predict that Suzie will be receiving a consequence soon, as she has given repeated indicators that she does not currently possess the skills to meet the expectation in the context of a classroom. Let's be clear, this is not a question of whether or not Suzie possesses the physical ability to raise her hand; it is about whether or not she possesses the behavioral skills to do it.

In the *correct* approach, the teacher moves away from the rush to exacerbate the problem and toward the learning opportunity. The teacher reminds the student of the desired outcome and the threat of consequence is not as prevalent. The language sounds something like, "Suzie, please remember that it is important to raise your hand when you have a contribution to make. Please stop calling out and interrupting." This seems to be a kinder, gentler approach to the issue and offers some strategy as a learning tool by reminding her of the expectation. However, there is still no connection to the bigger, desirable outcome.

In the *connect* approach, the teacher is not thinking about consequences but is totally immersed in the learning opportunity the calling-out challenge presents. The language sounds something like, "Suzie, let's remember what we talked about as being a demonstration of respect in this class. (Suzie responds with needing to raise her hand.) That's correct! I know that sometimes you get excited to share and I appreciate your good ideas, but we all need to remember the importance of respect in this classroom." In this situation, the teacher intentionally connects the desired behavior to an important expectation in the classroom. The teacher reminds Suzie of the need to exhibit the right behavior and provides an opportunity for her to demonstrate that she knows it. I know that some will be wondering if, in the connect approach, there ever is a consequence for repeated misbehavior. The answer is yes, provided the teacher couples the consequence with a teaching opportunity (such as in the dialogue demonstrated with Suzie in the *connect* phase above). In general, the connect approach results in enhanced teacher-student relationships as a result of teachers putting more emphasis on their role as instructors and less on their role as judges.

STORY

Greg Wolcott, the assistant superintendent for teaching and learning in Woodridge, Illinois, is one of the most positive educators I have encountered in my travels. He has an unshakeable belief in the ability of each student under his watch to succeed, and he works with educators to convey that message. One way he shares this message is by suggesting that every student comes into the classroom with his or her own strengths, talents, opportunities for growth, resources, and yearnings (STORY). When teachers know each student's STORY, they can offer feedback tailored to that student.

Strengths

Every student has strengths, and it's up to the adults to both recognize them and help the student leverage them in his or her school career. The strengths are as unique as each student, which makes this challenging for teachers, but the benefits are significant. Seeing students through their strengths rather than their deficits opens up opportunities for teachers to leverage those strengths while developing students' proficiency in other areas.

Talents

While *strength* refers to the ability to provide a quality performance in a specific activity, *talents* are naturally occurring behaviors that have the potential to develop into strengths. Not all talents are viewed the same. I have dropped by skateboard parks and marveled at the skills of the youngsters there. My amazement is tinged with some measure of disappointment, as often these students are absent from or disenfranchised by their schools. They are labeled as "not interested in learning," which could not be further from the truth. If you've ever seen a trick performed by a skater, you should be aware that the finished product you are witnessing came after lots of learning—most of it painful! Leveraging a talent to create a strength—in this case tapping into how a student learns—allows every student to achieve success and every teacher to provide more tailored feedback.

Opportunities for Growth

What can teachers do to provide students with environments where growth is not only possible but also achievable? Knowing students' strengths and talents is a start, and putting them in situations where they can leverage their strengths will continue their growth. All students should have growth opportunities during their months in school and be further along after each school year. For some, the steps might be small (as they build confidence as learners), while others may take larger steps that reflect their readiness.

Resources

Not all students have access to the same resources, be they financial, material, or human (family and friends), but this should not be a limiting factor during their time at school. Teachers should ensure that all expectations are achievable during school time and with school resources so that students with limited resources are not unfairly disadvantaged when they leave school at the end of the day.

Yearnings

Every student is a success story waiting to be told. Students all have a desire for success and need to know it is possible. However, some students will need the opportunity to develop the requisite skills for success. I believe every student in school today could respond to these three questions.

1. What do you know (about this topic)?
2. What don't you know (about this topic)?
3. What would you like to know (on this topic)?

In responding to these questions, students reveal what is important to them, and this will help the teacher shape feedback as students work toward the desired outcomes. Rushing to make assumptions about what students know, don't know, and would like to know creates less targeted instruction and depersonalizes the learning.

Maddie's STORY

To illustrate this technique, let's consider the example of a teacher, Ms. Morrison, who discovered the STORY of one of her students, Maddie.

◆ **Strengths:** Ms. Morrison spent time the first three days getting to know all of her students. She started by administering the VIA Institute on Character (www.viacharacter.org) strengths inventory and found out that Maddie's top strengths were in the areas of love, kindness, and leadership.

◆ **Talents:** Next, Ms. Morrison became a student of her students by watching for their individual tendencies throughout the school day. She noticed that Maddie was always happy and energetic, had great oral language abilities, and always walked her brother to his classroom.

◆ **Opportunities for growth:** Having closely observed Maddie, Ms. Morrison took note that Maddie suffered from a lack of persistence, frequently giving up on activities when they became overly challenging, and not tackling difficult tasks. This included reading books at challenging levels.

◆ **Resources:** Based on surveys sent home and meeting Maddie's parents, Ms. Morrison learned that Maddie had many resources at her disposal. Both parents were actively involved in her learning, and she didn't lack for food, attention, or love (some of Maslow's basic needs) on a daily basis.

◆ **Yearnings:** Ms. Morrison spent several minutes talking with Maddie about her love of learning and her passions and goals. She quickly learned that Maddie wanted to be a teacher when she grew up.

Based on the data collected and anecdotal information, Ms. Morrison felt she had a good understanding of Maddie and her STORY. Ms. Morrison then went to work developing a peer-tutoring program that would allow Maddie the opportunity to begin reading more challenging books followed by teaching and retelling them to younger female students. By utilizing Maddie's oral language strengths, her passion for teaching others, and her leadership skills, Ms. Morrison was able to develop an effective way to increase the level and difficulty of the texts Maddie read while leveraging some of Maddie's identified strengths. Within weeks, Maddie had increased not only her reading level but also her persistence, which helped her become a more confident student, ready to tackle the challenges she faced.

The Four-to-One Praise Ratio

Praise from teachers should communicate approval for the demonstration of desired outcomes. Researchers Hill M. Walker, Elizabeth Ramsey, and Frank M. Gresham (2004) suggest that the ratio of praise to criticism and reprimands should be at least four to one, and higher if possible. They suggest that praise be "immediate, frequent, enthusiastic, descriptive, varied, and should involve eye contact" (p. 72). While students who struggle with appropriate behaviors may not immediately respond to praise (and may even react negatively based on previous negative interactions with the adults in their lives), the positive impact of praise will eventually increase. Wesley C. Becker, Siegfried Engelmann, and Don R. Thomas (1975) look at the reverse impact and chronicle what happens when praise is removed and criticism is increased. After withdrawing praise from a classroom, off-task behavior increased from 8.7 percent to 25.5 percent. When the rate of criticism was increased, off-task behavior increased from 25.5 percent to 31.2 percent, with over 50 percent off-task behavior on some days.

It's clear that building a positive learning community requires an emphasis on authentic, meaningful, and personalized praise that engages students in their growth. One question that emerges, which is frequently presented as pushback for not engaging in praise, revolves around whether or not students will become conditioned to praise and then not respond in the absence of praise. In other words, will students become so conditioned that receiving praise will be the only way they will respond? Jane A. G. Kise (2014) addresses this dichotomy by suggesting educators need to look at the advantages of both polarities. She says, "We are both searching for the truth about how to help students succeed and for public policy that can bring that truth into reality" (p. 26). It's really an *and proposition* instead of an *or choice*. When considering how much praise is too much or if teachers are overindulging students, first address the purpose for the action, monitor the impact, and check for student growth. If students are immobilized—if they won't demonstrate the desired behavior in the absence of praise—then consider altering the frequency or identifying target students who might need a different approach.

Feedback From Students to Teachers

The examples below are highly effective tools in gathering feedback from students. The challenge that teachers must brace themselves for is that students will often present information in a very raw, unfiltered fashion. This is a key time when presuming positive intention will allow teachers to take the feedback as valuable information and not as a personal attack.

Tell Them From Me

The "Tell Them From Me" student survey (www.tellthemfromme.com) is web based and measures student engagement through the students' direct participation and voice. The survey aims to help schools promote and monitor practices that positively affect students' sense of belonging, well-being, and, ultimately, achievement. There is a direct link between students' attitudes toward learning and their academic success. Engagement and learning have an important and symbiotic relationship—engagement leads to learning, and learning leads to engagement.

Let's look at some data collected from student responses to the survey and frame these responses around some of the content covered in this book. The data, provided by principal Richard Payne (personal communication, April 12, 2016), are organized by elementary and secondary grade spans with the comments as they were provided, including any grammatical or spelling errors.

Elementary School Examples

Please tell us some of the things you really like about your school.

- *I also like it because I am accepted for who I am and usually don't have any troubles making friends.*

- *I really like that the teachers help us out with not school related problems.*

What is one important change you have found out about yourself this year?

- *I am fully capable of getting in trouble but also capable of being good.*

- *I found that I was starting to be more open about my feelings to my teacher about stuff that goes on in my life.*

Note that these first two questions seek information about the DNA (dreams, needs, and abilities) of the students to help them connect with the desired outcomes. The next question highlights the importance of engaging students in the learning.

Please tell us some of the things you really like about your school, or things that would make it even better.

◆ *I like my school but some time I think we learn stuff that wont help*
us in the real word like in math all the stratages are for nothing.

Secondary School Examples

The need to establish strong caring relationships is significant at the secondary
level. Listening to students and responding to what they share builds capacity.

In what ways have you contributed to the positive culture at our school?

◆ *I participate in every club and activity in school because i believe*
if you want change in your school or community you should speak
about it and let people know what you think.

◆ *I am a leader in our junior high/high school groups, and I have*
helped teach grade 1,2,3, and 4 children to read during lunch
hours.

We are hoping that there is at least one staff member that you can go to with concerns or problems. If there isn't, please tell us what stops you from approaching someone for help.

◆ *I do not go to someone for help because I am too embarrassed and*
in the past I have gone to a teacher and every time they told me to
ignore it so I stopped asking teachers for help.

Please tell us some of the things you really like about your school, or things that would make it even better.

◆ *I enjoy when the whole school goes into their groups and competes.*
It helped me create friendships with people from other grades that I
wouldn't have if this activity wasn't created.

◆ *i think that homework and tests should be limited to one class a*
day because for students with after school jobs it is hard to get home
from work at around 10–10:30 and still do a minimum of an
hours worth of homework then do other things to get ready for the
next day at school and still get enough sleep to be focused in class the
next day.

◆ *Also some of the teachers need to drastically change their way of*
teaching cause no one is learning from them. Teaching by the
textbook, reading it over as a class will not help us learn better.

Principal Richard Payne offers this feedback on the value of this information gathered:

> *It took about two years to start getting what we believed was meaning-ful data from the students—once they started treating it more seriously and began to recognize that we were truly interested in their input on issues that were relevant to them. We find the responses to the open-ended questions to be the most revealing. The data tell a story of our journey the last four years (particularly with respect to the issues of bullying and sense of belonging). The student feedback that we gather helps us monitor our progress, and informs our decision-making as we move forward. (personal communication, April 12, 2016.)*

I Wish My Teacher Knew

Every year, Denver teacher Kyle Schwartz passes out sticky notes to her third-grade students and asks them to complete the sentence, "I wish my teacher knew . . ." The responses are honest and occasionally gut wrenching as they reveal some things the teacher might not otherwise have tapped into. Other teachers wishing to know more about their students may like to employ this same technique. The more teachers know about their students and their backgrounds, the more they can connect with them and help them realize their personal success stories. How might a message such as "I wish my teacher knew sometimes my reading log is not signed because my mom is not around a lot" shift a teacher's thinking when it's time to determine whether or not a student is achieving the desired outcome? Feedback using this method can also be helpful to let teachers know whether a particular intervention or teaching strategy is resonating with students.

Indigenous Student Success

In Canada, the term "Indigenous" includes First Nations, Métis, and Inuit peo-ple. Kerry Mahlman is the district principal for First Nations students in School District #46 (Sunshine Coast) in the province of British Columbia. The success rates for this demographic of students—defined as the six-year completion rate that identifies the percentage of grade 8 students who attain a high school diploma in that time period—continues to grow and outpaces the provincial average each year. The last year of available data shows the provincial average at 63 percent (67 percent for females and 60 percent for males), which continues the upward trend, while the district average is at 72 percent (80 percent for females and 64 percent for males); this also continues an upward trend. As Mahlman notes, "Fifteen years ago the rate was 12 percent. The students and schools have come a long way!" (personal communication, August 30, 2016).

In trying to identify what components of effective practice might have led to this success so that other jurisdictions might reap similar benefits, Mahlman has identified the following six key strategies:

1. **A systemwide commitment:** The entire school organization needs to be committed to making a difference for Indigenous students and understand why this commitment is necessary. This works best if interventions should occur across an entire state or province, or at least an entire school district, with the support of every person in a leadership position within that district. In this, teachers and support staff are key leaders. The most significant influences on a student's success in school are the teachers and support staff members working with the student every day. There is shared responsibility for student learning, and everyone moves toward being a community of practice that will make a difference for Indigenous students. And the added bonus? What is good for Indigenous students is most often good for all students.

   Which individuals have the shared responsibility for Indigenous student success in a school district, and should thus be part of the commitment to achieve results?

   - The Indigenous community (non-traditional partners as well as those agencies that typically overlap or interact with the school system)
   - The Board of Education
   - Superintendent and assistant superintendent
   - District staff—secretary, treasurer, directors, district principals, and coordinators
   - Principals, vice principals, and teachers
   - Support staff
   - Parents
   - Students
   - The broader community

2. **An inclusionary approach:** All students receive the cultural teachings. In certain cases, this has almost eliminated overt racism among the students, deepened the understanding and respect among students and staff, heightened the value of diversity and the students' sense of social justice, and increased the cultural pride of Indigenous students.

3. **An early start:** Programs and services start with early learning and kindergarten, then continue all the way to graduation. Educators know every student and family, and place a key emphasis on long-term relationships.

4. **A welcoming environment:** Schools work to be welcoming and culturally responsive and to create a sense of belonging and cultural safety. Indigenous culture is a presence in the school—Indigenous students see themselves reflected in the physical surroundings, in the school culture, in the learning, and in staff.

5. **An eye on progress:** Teachers monitor the spiral of indicators that loosely follows age and developmental stages and characteristics of educational programs and, when needed, implement appropriate student-centered intervention based on the pyramid of intervention.

6. **A positive future vision:** Perhaps a bigger factor than we realize, success is greater than the education system alone. Indigenous people themselves are gaining momentum in social change, social justice, and health, and in a renewed sense of identity, culture, and well-being (healing). The community and especially the youth have to have a vision for a positive personal future. That vision of the future has to include valuing an education, and people must regard the education system offered as safe, respectful, responsive to the needs of Indigenous people, meaningful, and relevant. Otherwise, no matter what the system does, Indigenous people will not engage.

Success is possible for all of the students that come to our schools today. Engaging students in their learning outcomes, soliciting and encouraging their voice, and establishing them as partners in their learning will help educators achieve the breakthroughs necessary to reach the goal of all students experiencing high levels of success. As Mahlman concludes, "There is still a long way to go, but what success we have had so far is based on the cumulative impact of a number of factors" (personal communication, August 20, 2016). Solutions are achieved when teams of educators believe they can be.

Using Feedback to Close Behavioral Gaps

Appropriate feedback becomes particularly important when teachers take an approach that involves the correction and closing of any behavioral or academic gaps. The challenge with giving feedback in these situations often stems from the dual desires of rushing to consequence as a punishment for the behavior versus taking the time to actually teach it, as John Hattie and Helen Timperley (2007) suggest:

> *Feedback has no effect in a vacuum; to be powerful in its effect, there must be a learning context to which feedback is addressed. It is but part of the teaching process and is that which happens second—after a student has responded to initial instruction—when information is provided regarding some aspect(s) of the student's task performance. (p. 82)*

If students have never been taught the desired behavioral outcomes, or if educators expect that they ought to know or should have learned the expectations elsewhere, then there should be little surprise that misbehavior continues and that the consequences have seemingly little impact. A consequence of the rush to punishment may actually be an increase in negative behavior. What may seem like a consequence to the teacher may actually reinforce the very behavior the teacher is trying to discourage. Hattie and Timperley (2007) state, "If feedback is directed at the right level, it can assist students to comprehend, engage, or develop effective strategies to process the information intended to be learned" (p. 104). Feedback must build on something, and educators must be willing to build on the skills students already have as they facilitate development of the desired skills. If the intended outcome is regular demonstration of the desired behavior, teachers will need to use structured, personalized feedback as a vehicle to achieve that outcome.

 ## A Strategy to Consider

To put the four-to-one praise ratio into practice, the teacher should prepare forty pieces of unpopped popcorn at the start of the day. Each time the teacher observes a student practicing good behavior, he or she then provides reinforcement to that same student for following behavioral expectations and places one kernel in the right pocket. The teacher places another kernel in the left pocket every time he or she provides behavioral correction to a student. At the end of the day, the teacher counts how many kernels are in his or her pockets and then calculates a ratio based on that count. Teachers should strive for the four-to-one praise-to-criticism ratio mentioned previously (see page 51), but should allow some time to achieve this desired ratio.

Points Worth Remembering

- Positive reinforcement yields the desired results that negative consequences never can.
- Timely and specific feedback is a critical component of sound assessment.
- The direct to correct to connect approach helps enhance relationships and teach desired behaviors.
- Every student has a STORY (strengths, talents, opportunities for growth, resources, and yearnings). Teachers should learn each student's STORY and share theirs.
- The four-to-one ratio of positive-to-negative interactions yields great benefits.
- Feedback from students and hearing their voices are key components to developing effective teaching methods.

DATA-DRIVEN DECISIONS

Key 4: Data-Driven Decisions

Various formative assessments are in place to track behavior and academic progress. The information collected is specific enough to generate general baseline data and patterns of behavior for individual students. Using these data, teachers adjust, modify, or reteach specific skills in proactive ways.

In our daily lives, it would be almost impossible to make decisions without first accessing data. We plan activities using weather data, buy food for those activities based on grocery store prices, and fuel up for the trip based on who has the best gasoline prices. If someone falls ill on the trip, we may need to see a doctor who we will expect to use data to advise us on the next course of action. Yet, in education, teachers often make decisions based entirely on supposition and intuition, reacting to what appears on the surface and prescribing an outcome that may not relate to changing the cause. It is akin to spinning a roulette wheel of treatment options based on a general malaise, rather than having a doctor gather and interpret data.

Case Study: Data-Driven Decisions Improve Student Outcomes

Garth Larson is the director of learning for the Winneconne Community School District in Wisconsin. He shares this story from his first year of teaching:

> *Harold was struggling to meet classroom expectations (collectively agreed upon). I thought I needed to be the strong first year teacher and kick the student out of my classroom (notice I thought it was my classroom at the time and was not yet fully thinking of it as our classroom). This happened three days in a row, and I soon realized that kicking Harold out of the classroom was not changing the behavior and there was no learning occurring while he was spending his time in the office. On the third day of his removal from the classroom, I was in charge of the weight room that night. Although Harold struggled to stay eligible for sports, he would still come to the weight room after school. I saw my opportunity for him to recognize I wanted to see him do well and that I was an advocate for his education. He was on the bench press and I slowly walked over to him and said, "How many are we going to get?" He told me the number and I said, "Okay, let's do this!" He went on to lift several sets with me spotting him as he went. We didn't talk a lot and certainly didn't talk about what had happened in class. However, the next morning when Harold walked into our classroom, he was a different student. He was actively engaged in our discussions, never had a behavior problem the rest of the year, and later indicated that he really enjoyed being in our class. (personal communication, December 20, 2015)*

Had the teacher stuck with his first intuition and just kept kicking the student out of class, would he have addressed the problem? In the rush to establish his role, did the teacher ignore some compelling data—in this case perhaps related to a sense of belonging or connectedness? In building a connection, the teacher was able to achieve the desired behavioral outcomes in class, and the student felt like he had someone who knew him and was on his side. If teachers ignore the information at hand, they default to easy solutions that often preclude achieving the desired outcome.

The Most Important Three-Letter Word—*Yet*

Think of any group of thirty people whose only commonality is their age. Would it be reasonable to expect that each member of this group has the same ability in mathematics? That they all read at the same level with the same fluency, comprehension, and vocabulary? Or that they all have the same writing ability and can produce brilliance on any topic? Would they all demonstrate the same self-regulation in social situations? I think we can readily agree it would be folly to make those broad assumptions. However, this is what teachers routinely do in classrooms. They expect every fourteen-year-old to be able to handle all grade 9 content and behavioral outcomes when clearly this will not be the case.

I do not intend to suggest that educators should not have expectations for certain levels of knowledge or requisite behaviors. We can establish *need to knows* across all these areas and recognize readily that in order to function as adults, all citizens need to know how to read, write, do basic computation, and have some self-regulation. The challenge is when we expect everyone to hit the marks at the same time and in the same way.

When the data indicate a student has not achieved the desired outcome, teachers need to employ the most important three-letter word in education—*yet*. Students have not met proficiency—*yet*. This indicates there is still the possibility for them to achieve that goal and that teachers are committed to helping them achieve it. This is an absolute requirement for anything a teacher describes as essential learning or need to know. There are no other options available, and holding students and teachers accountable for achieving the desired outcomes has to be part of every classroom. However, the achievement does not have to happen all at once.

Data Versus Evidence

Teachers in modern classrooms have an almost unprecedented access to data. It's all around the classroom and in every interaction. Douglas Reeves (2009) points out that schools and districts are drowning in data (information accumulated on a variety of topics or outcomes but never used to drive change), but thirsty for evidence (actionable information that aligns with the purpose established, accompanied by questions like, Is the strategy working? How do you know?). Karen Engels (2015) states, "By relying on standardized data, teachers will lose the intimate knowledge of each student that's so crucial to our ability to advance skills" (p. 76). How teachers react and respond to the evidence they collect becomes the framework for either student growth or stagnation.

One way in which teachers drown in data is by using data as a hammer when the numbers or letters are simply used to rank and sort. They are absolutely convinced that 93 is better than 87, which is better than 75, and so on, and they make this assertion without even knowing what went into the 93 or 87 or 75. The variation in absolute numbers from teacher to teacher alone renders the comparison a moot point, but still, teachers persist in their reliance on such numbers. When the teacher is reliant simply on a number (regardless of how and despite the variation that might occur classroom to classroom) then that is how they view their student. They exclude any other factors outside the students or any abilities within the student that might not have been visible in the number collection. Data as a hammer yield very little information about the student and even less about potential next steps.

On the opposite end of the spectrum are the teachers who are reluctant to use data. They may be fearful of misinterpretation of raw scores or worry about low scores reflecting on them personally. While I believe that teacher judgment is a very effective tool, it must be paired with high-quality assessment practice to validate the judgment. Some of the reluctance to effectively use data, ironically, stems from the misuse of data! Relying simply on judgment, and especially when that judgment is not grounded with other colleagues, without the demonstration makes the decision rendered harder to justify. Using judgment as a starting point to build knowledge of a student that can then be articulated in concert with quality assessment results is sound practice that promotes the best student outcomes.

These occur when teachers use an educated combination of data and teacher judgment—something I'm labeling *evidence.* In contrast to using data as a hammer, as discussed earlier, these teachers use data as a flashlight. This means converting numbers to evidence that speaks to both the accomplishment of a learning target and a measure of the effectiveness of the chosen instructional strategy. For example, the evidence provided by an early screening of student literacy may indicate that the current cohort of grade 3 students is the lowest-functioning group the teacher has ever had. This conclusion cries out for action on the teacher's part. The teacher cannot implement last year's Tier 1 universal instruction because he or she doesn't have last year's students. Instead, the teacher must adapt Tier 1 for the current group of students. Once teachers use data as flashlight, they clearly illuminate what steps need to happen next. Combine this use of data with sound teacher judgment and it is the blueprint for widespread student success.

Teacher judgment is an excellent tool or skill that is highly undervalued. Like any good tool, however, it needs regular use to maximize the benefits. Teacher judgment is neither the quick response to a first hunch nor ignoring all the clues in favor of an assessment response. Instead, *teacher judgment* is about utilizing perceptions (hunches) and framing them positively to achieve a better outcome. Achieving better remediation and building skills expected of students occurs when teachers examine the context of an exhibited behavior. See the section on the ABC analysis tool on page 66 for more details.

Engels (2015) states of teacher judgment, "An overreliance on scientific measures and a devaluation of teacher expertise will have deleterious consequences for the whole profession as new teachers enter a field that doesn't push them" (p. 76). There is great value in teacher knowledge and awareness that aligns more with the actions Garth Larson took in the case study on page 60 (building a connection with the student) than with the actions he began with (a rush to consequence without knowing the reasons behind the student's behavior). In that situation, the use of evidence rather than data made all the difference to the outcome for the student.

Data to Close the Gaps

Any data or evidence collected by a teacher should lead to teacher decisions to help close behavioral or academic gaps. When data indicate that a student does not meet proficiency on essential academic learning targets, the teacher should immediately begin a course of action to remedy the situation. Failing to take the necessary steps to close the gap in a student's academic progress is tantamount to condoning failure. It indicates a mindset of focusing on content that is *nice to know* or *helpful to know*, instead of the crucial *need to know* that leads to success. If this is not the intent, then educators must be willing to do what is necessary to reach the preferred outcomes.

Just as with academic learning deficits, students also experience behavioral learning gaps when they have not developed behavioral skills appropriate for their age level. These gaps can likewise be identified using data. Consider the collected data on the behavioral front. The teacher can observe, record, and analyze the student's behavior across a variety of settings by considering, Is the inappropriate behavior content based? Does it depend on the time of day? Day of the week? Does a particular instructional strategy or activity precede the behavior? The first step in this process is to gather baseline data to establish the purpose of the behavior and to begin to formulate plans for remediation. This may take three to five days and should look at a behavior's frequency, the length of time the behavior occurs, and the behavior's severity. From these data, a remediation plan must be defined, monitored, and altered based on the information gathered.

There are two questions to ponder after implementing a plan to evaluate its efficacy: (1) Is the plan (intervention) working? (2) How do we ensure ongoing success? Clarity around the required learning targets and a deep commitment to taking the necessary steps will ensure actualized behavioral interventions. Rather than condoning failure, successful teachers spend their time and energy acknowledging the diversity in their classrooms and the uniqueness of each student and using data to close gaps, thereby ensuring every student clears the bar—or better!

Assessment Strategies at the Classroom Level

The best assessments serve as sources of meaningful information. The question teachers should ask themselves is, "Did I teach this content effectively, with a strategy that led to learning for all?" Formative assessments involve checking for understanding and are the most important and useful for gathering student data. Teachers can use exit slips, brief quizzes, thumbs up or thumbs down, and whiteboards (to name a few) to gather information on where students are and where they need to go next. The analysis of this information requires courage and a willingness to step away from the "I taught them; they just didn't learn" narrative relied upon for far too long. Thomas R. Guskey (2003) states that most teachers "recognize that their effectiveness is not defined on the basis of what they do as teachers but rather on what their students are able to do."

The step that immediately follows gathering data and data analysis is perhaps the most critical: teachers must follow with corrective instruction. Recall the direct to correct to connect continuum from chapter 4 (page 47). The power of assessment in promoting learning and understanding relies on the corrective procedures teachers follow to close the gap. Teachers must let go of the entrenched viewpoint that students should receive just a one-time opportunity to demonstrate the desired skill (such as a test at the end of a unit). Rather, once teachers have gathered information, analyzed it, and embarked on a new strategy to facilitate learning for those who didn't understand the first time, there must be a second chance for students to demonstrate that they have acquired the skills. Reeves (2005), in his chapter in *On Common Ground*, offers a clear metaphor when he talks about the difference between a physical exam (formative use) and an autopsy (summative use):

> *Physicals at a certain point in life can be an uncomfortable ordeal but, on the whole, they are preferable to and less intrusive than autopsies. . . . The keys to assessment for learning—the physical rather than the autopsy—are consistency, timeliness, and differentiation. (p. 53)*

One final practice teachers should consider in their classroom assessment toolbox is observation. Work to ensure that students are comfortable by walking around and sitting with them in their groups. Move away from the "sage on the stage" role to a "guide on the side" practice. This will afford teachers insights they cannot always garner from the front of the class as they gather data on individual students. Then, use these data to see if students are making sense of the content, struggling with the learning activity, interacting with others, or receiving feedback from peers. On this latter point, Graham Nuthall's (2007) work mentioned in chapter 4 suggests 80 percent of feedback students receive about their work in primary school comes from other students and 80 percent of this student-to-student feedback is incorrect. Taking the time to move around the classroom allows for immediate intervention and clarification from the teacher, rather than from peers. Teachers can employ an observation tool like the one found in figure 5.1 (page 66) to serve as a repository of what they notice.

Data-Collection Toolbox for Teachers

I am hoping that the chapters thus far have provided some insights, opportunities for reflections, and new tools for your toolbox. When it comes to data collection, it's very important to have tools that yield quality, actionable evidence. This next section provides some of those tools.

Reading Observation

Student name: _____   Date: _____

Book title: _____

Reads with fluency: Yes or No

Reads with expression: Yes or No

Decoding strategies observed:

Evidence of text comprehension:

Mathematics Observation

Student name: _____   Date: _____

Mathematics problem or exercise:

Skill being worked on:

Mathematics strategies observed:

Evidence of student mastery:

Figure 5.1: Sample observation form for a reading and mathematics class.

*Visit **go.SolutionTree.com/behavior** for a free reproducible version of this figure.*

ABC: An Early Analysis Tool

ABC is a direct-observation tool that teachers can use to collect information about why a student is not demonstrating proficiency for a behavior. The *A* refers to the antecedent (the event, activity, and environment) immediately before the problem behavior. The *B* refers to the behavior the teacher observes, and the *C* refers to the consequence of the behavior. The teacher can complete a simple chart like figure 5.2 (page 68) as he or she develops a potential intervention strategy.

Let's look at an example. The teacher calls on Elaine to be the first reader in class. Elaine slams her book shut and throws it off her desk. The teacher then sends Elaine to the office. In this case, the antecedent (A) is the request made by the teacher. Perhaps Elaine is a poor reader and does not want this exposed to her peers. Perhaps she is shy and uncomfortable with public speaking. Perhaps it is the time of day when she is not "school ready." Elaine's behavior (B) is to slam and throw her book. Remember, all behavior occurs for one of two reasons: to get something or to avoid something. Her consequence (C) is removal from class. The teacher needs to ask herself, "Is this consequence having the desired effect?" If it is not (that is, if the misbehavior still occurs regularly), then the teacher must have a next step to pursue. In this case, the *function* of Elaine's behavior is to escape the classroom and avoid the request. There is another way to process this challenge while ensuring the success of the long-term objective (oral reading) and closing another gap—Elaine's behavior.

In this scenario, the teacher asks Elaine to perform a reasonable task. Let's assume this is not the first time the teacher has seen Elaine's response (that is, the teacher is prepared with baseline data). The teacher should build an appropriate intervention plan from there. She may have noticed that Elaine might need some early warning about the upcoming request to read. The response might be to pick the section and allow Elaine to practice in advance. If the challenge relates to some other environmental concern (time of day or day of the week, for example), the teacher can use the same approach. If Elaine has a similar response following these interventions, the teacher could engage in an alternative response that does not result in removal and task avoidance. For example, a quiet zone within the classroom could be employed. Think about how much time a student misses in high-quality instruction and engagement when the teacher sends the student to the office. Often, these are students who already have considerable gaps in their learning and need more instructional time. Using a signal card system, Elaine could let the teacher know when she is green (good to go), yellow (starting to slow), or red (ready to blow) before acting out. The use of an alternative learning environment (a colleague's classroom or a quiet space in the classroom) could also help Elaine and avoid involving the office. These interventions require context and the responses will vary from student to

Date	Time	Antecedent	Behavior	Consequence	Possible Function (Why is this behavior occurring?)

Figure 5.2: The ABC direct-observation tool.

Visit go.SolutionTree.com/behavior for a free reproducible version of this figure.

student. However, the ultimate goal remains the same—helping Elaine close the gaps in her learning, both academic and behavioral.

Event Recording

Event recording is similar to the Strategy to Consider described in chapter 4 (page 57) where a teacher counts the number of times a particular behavior is demonstrated with unpopped popcorn kernels. With event recording, teachers keep track of behaviors with tally marks. This is a good option if the desired outcome is to simply track the number of times a behavior occurs throughout the day. This method is not a good option when the behavior is so frequent that tracking becomes a challenge.

Interval Recording

Interval recording involves tallying behaviors as they occur over a set time period. The teacher should define a time period for observation, divide that time into equal intervals, select a method of recording, and define the behavior they will be observing in clear terms so recording is accurate. The challenge with this method is to ensure accuracy with the interval times. Using a timer could help make sure teaching time is not lost in the eagerness to record data. If possible, utilizing another objective observer is the best option.

Momentary Time Sampling

Momentary time sampling involves observing whether a behavior occurs or not during a specified time period, and then recording the data at the end of the time period. This method is effective for groups of students and for recording more than one behavior. However, it is only effective when done repeatedly over the course of a class at fixed (every four minutes) or varying (three, then seven, then five minutes) intervals.

Duration Recording

Duration recording documents the amount of time a student spends engaging in a behavior. This method is best for recording behaviors that have a clear beginning and end. This is not a good method for frequent behaviors (unless a second person is also recording) or for behaviors that do not have clear start and stop points.

Instructional Agility

Tom Schimmer (2016) describes *instructional agility* as the capacity of a teacher to decide on and make any necessary maneuvers required by gathered information in as short a time as possible during instructional delivery. Earlier in this chapter, I discussed the importance of formatively assessing students to identify any gaps (see Data to Close the Gaps, page 63). The information gathered by the teacher must be used, or have the potential to be used, in an instructional intervention in order to close the gaps.

In my chapter in *The Teacher as Assessment Leader*, I describe this back-and-forth cycle:

> *Assessment and instruction are almost seamless in this ongoing exchange of information between teacher and student. Your role is to make frequent environmental scans to collect formal evidence, such as assignments, exams, or homework, and informal evidence, such as the questions students may ask, their comments during group work, or even their confused expressions. The analysis of this evidence informs your practice and provides critical information as to next steps.* (Hierck, 2009, p. 252)

Responding with immediacy to information allows teachers to work in partnership with students in the moment and often when the learning gap is the smallest. Ignoring the information, hoping students can close the gap on their own, or waiting until frustration has overwhelmed them seem like less desirable options. Gathering information in daily practice is valuable when that information drives next steps. In the absence of daily data collection, teachers may resort to gathering information only at an endpoint or in a summative fashion as required. This, however, is a return to using data as a hammer. Information gathering, when used effectively, is too valuable to waste by leaving interventions to the end of the unit, term, or semester.

As with all of the best strategies in education, it's important not to take instructional agility out of context. Schimmer (2016) suggests that some might wrongly assume that instructional agility is akin to instructional freedom, thereby granting license for teachers to ignore standards, curriculum documents, or pacing guides. However, the intent of instructional agility is not to eliminate the precision gained from these documents but instead to pair it with the flexibility to adapt to students' demonstrated capacities in an effort to improve overall outcomes and not just assess them.

A Strategy to Consider

Grade 5 student Maddie offers this suggestion for teachers to consider as they try to minimize disruptions during transitions and build cooperative skills: "Kids love classroom rewards and recognition when they have done well going from art, music, and PE back to the class or when they line up well. It's a good way to demonstrate teamwork." These rewards may vary from grade level to grade level, may be classroom based or schoolwide, may be theme driven ("This month we will be looking for examples of respectful behavior"), and may be either extrinsic (tokens, tickets, compliments, pats on the back) or intrinsic (pride in their work). It's the recognition that is key, and a consistent approach by the teacher will yield the greatest impact.

Points Worth Remembering

- Educators have considerable access to data, but they must avoid being data rich, information poor.
- The most important three-letter word in education is *yet*.
- Teacher judgment plus data is more effective evidence than either teacher judgment or data alone.
- Teachers should use data as a flashlight rather than as a hammer.
- Data should help teachers close gaps in student learning—behavioral and academic.
- ABC is a great analysis tool for tracking the antecedent, behavior, and consequence for students demonstrating problem behaviors or lack of proficiency.
- Other methods of tracking information on students include:
    - Event recording
    - Interval recording
    - Momentary time sampling
    - Duration recording
- Instructional agility is teachers' capacity to make necessary instructional shifts in real time. It allows teachers to respond to data with immediacy and improve outcomes for students.

DIFFERENTIATION AND ENRICHMENT

Key 5: Differentiation and Enrichment

A continuum of strategies, developed and aligned with classroom expectations, exists to support teachers in working to improve students' individual and group behavior. The focus of the strategies is to help the students learn to behave and succeed in the classroom. Alternative strategies are in place for escalating levels of misbehavior.

Differentiation is one of the concepts in education that has a myriad of definitions and intentionality surrounding it. It is the perfect example of what Michael Fullan (2005) was referring to when he wrote, "Terms travel easily . . . but the meaning of the underlying concepts does not" (p. 67). It may be easier to state what differentiation is *not* as a prelude to structuring a positive view of the work. Differentiation is not like following a recipe, implementing an instructional strategy, or even doing only what a teacher does when he or she has time. It is also definitely not amending your teaching only to be slower and louder. Differentiation demands that teachers know their students well (think DNA) so that they can provide each one with experiences and tasks that will improve that student's learning. It means that teachers observe and understand the differences and similarities among students and use this information to plan instruction.

To fully appreciate the power of this philosophy, I turn to the leader in this work, Carol Ann Tomlinson (2000), who outlines a set of beliefs that really shape the outcomes for students.

◆ Students who are the same age differ in their readiness to learn, their interests, their styles of learning, their experiences, and their life circumstances.

◆ The differences in students are significant enough to make a major impact on what students need to learn, the pace at which they need to learn it, and the support they need from teachers and others to learn it well.

◆ Students will learn best when supportive adults push them slightly beyond where they can work without assistance.

◆ Students will learn best when they can make a connection between the curriculum and their interests and life experiences.

◆ Students will learn best when learning opportunities are natural.

◆ Students are more effective learners when classrooms and schools create a sense of community in which students feel significant and respected.

◆ The central job of schools is to maximize the capacity of each student.

Differentiation must be an extension of high-quality instruction and curriculum design. Tomlinson (2000) reminds educators that differentiation is unlikely to happen for all students unless curriculum and instruction fit each individual, embrace student choice about what to learn and how, allow for the setting of learning goals, and connect with the experiences and interest of the individual. Teachers can differentiate on content, process, product, or environment. Here's a quick example of each.

1. **Content consists of facts, concepts, attitudes, and skills related to a subject or unit:** Teachers can differentiate content by using mathematics manipulatives with some, but not all, learners to help students understand a new idea or by using texts or novels at more than one reading level.

2. **Process is how the learner comes to make sense of, understand, and "own" the content:** Differentiating here can consist of providing varied options at differing levels of difficulty or based on differing student interests. Students might have choice in how or what they complete to show what they know.

3. **Product refers to the items a student can use to demonstrate what he or she has learned:** Students could choose, based on their learning style, the type of product they will submit (an oral report, a diorama, a written report, or a graphic organizer).

4. **Environment speaks to the layout of the classroom and includes the physical and psychological components:** Teachers could separate the students into groups to discuss the assignment.

Enrichment is an equally misunderstood concept and is, in many ways, akin to differentiation. In fact, enriching the learning of students through extension *is* a type of differentiation. Diane Heacox (2014) suggests, "Differentiated instruction is a way of thinking about teaching and learning" (p. 1), and this is often the goal of enrichment as well.

Like the differentiation definition, it is helpful to define enrichment by the things that it is *not*. Enrichment is not more of the same instruction, extra questions at the same level (this is poor planning or instructional design), or simply moving the student along the grade level in the content domain (which often creates more scheduling challenges). Rather, enrichment involves the learning opportunities and activities that engage students in developing their extended knowledge and skills. Enrichment extends the students' thinking, instead of just acknowledging it.

Enrichment is about stretching students, and the strategies are as varied as the students themselves. One suggested model, proposed by Donald J. Treffinger and Marion R. Sortore (1992), identifies four stages.

1. **Services for all students** incorporate some activities (including thinking skills training, independent projects, and exploratory activities) to challenge even the most gifted.

2. **Services for many students** include activities such as participation in academic competitions, clubs, and performing and visual arts, and curriculum compacting.

3. **Services for some students** include advanced classes, individual training in fine arts, and participation in special programs at universities.

4. **Services for a few students** include independent studies and professional mentorships.

While this model focuses on academic progression, it is equally important that teachers consider the behavioral growth required of students. It is incorrect to assume that a student's academic capacity to excel means that he or she will also excel in the behavioral domain. Gifted students are subject to the same life experiences, peer pressure, and societal influences as any other students. Once they leave the world of school, behaviors that may have seemed quirky in school could become problematic in their adult world. While I may enjoy watching the antics of the physicists on the television show *The Big Bang Theory*, I know the social foibles that seem humorous there can have a deeper and more negative impact for those young adults who were not engaged in learning positive behaviors while in school. In a later section of this chapter, we'll examine the rationale for supporting gifted students with strategies effective in producing positive behavioral outcomes.

Gathering and Responding to Evidence

Teachers need to gather evidence before making important instructional decisions or considering differentiation strategies for those students not yet attaining proficiency. Educators gather this evidence through sound assessment practice. As mentioned in chapter 5 (page 59), educators can gather evidence through a variety of formative approaches, from simple checks for understanding to well-designed pencil-and-paper assessments. It's the work done after the gathering and analyzing of the evidence—the response—that constitutes the critical next step.

Some models for teacher response are response to intervention (RTI), response to instruction and intervention (RTI²), multitiered systems of support (MTSS) and comprehensive student support systems (CSSS), to name a few. An introduction to RTI and MTSS is in the following section. The model teachers choose is not critical; rather, the important part is understanding the underpinnings of the work—the outcomes desired of students—and shaping classrooms around those outcomes. Jim Wright (2014) notes, "Teachers who believe that they can be effective interventionists and are energized to do so are far more likely to attain success than their reluctant colleagues who lack confidence in their ability to carry out that role" (p. 248). As Chris Weber and I contemplated the implications of RTI in the book *RTI Is a Verb*, we suggested, "It [RTI] demands action on the part of every educator on behalf of every student" (Hierck & Weber, 2014a, p. 179). It requires that teachers abandon the well-rehearsed narrative of excuse making and commit to do what is necessary to ensure that all students, during their watch, will experience growth. In order to effectively differentiate and enrich the learning experiences of all students, teachers need to gather evidence to plan the next steps. It is this personalization of the learning process that will lead to growth for all students.

RTI and MTSS: An Introduction to a Key Tool

RTI is one of the most common models for teachers to use when differentiating in the classroom. Implementing an RTI framework for behavior should mirror the familiar steps teachers might take with academic RTI. This approach allows teachers to respond to student needs more systematically and proactively. Within an RTI framework, students are engaged in the rich, deep learning experiences of Tier 1 instruction while receiving the necessary, targeted interventions to close achievement gaps and accelerate learning.

It's clear that some students will need more time and alternative approaches to reach proficiency. This is predictable. However, they do not need remedial instruction, removal from class, or watered-down expectations; they need Tier 2 support. Evidence-gathering tools (diagnostics, referrals, and so on) drive Tier 2 interventions. Tier 2 represents targeted interventions to help students master the desired outcomes not sufficiently learned at Tier 1.

Educators should provide intensive, individualized interventions for students with significant deficits (multiple years behind in foundational prerequisite skills like self-regulation, organization, empathy, and attentiveness). The goal of Tier 3 interventions is to accelerate learning through diagnostically driven support to close gaps, not to provide a separate but unequal (and often isolated) behavior experience. Thus, RTI shifts a school's response to struggling learners from a remediation model that too often masks learning needs to one of targeted interventions that promote accelerated learning and higher levels of achievement. A teacher's approach to RTI or MTSS must allow for Tier 1, Tier 2, *and* Tier 3.

When gathering evidence, the most important tier is the one that addresses all students. Teacher expectations for all students, their best instructional practice and design, and their instructional agility all begin at Tier 1. All classroom teachers provide lessons and coaching to define and teach specific prosocial skills (the expectations defined through actions). They also precorrect some students to use appropriate behaviors (if teachers can predict it, they can prevent it) and provide all students with opportunities to practice and be reinforced for those desired behaviors (redundancy builds fluency). It is only after the baseline expectations have been established and taught that teachers can begin to look at what else they might do for students not attaining proficiency.

If the evidence suggests some students might need additional supports, teachers should move to Tier 2 strategies. In general, students receiving this next layer of support (additional to what they are receiving at Tier 1) are exhibiting behaviors that are not harmful to themselves or others, but instead are disruptive to the learning environment. The intention is to work with students exhibiting similar struggles with additional time built into the school schedule. During this additional time with smaller groups, the interventions could include reteaching prosocial or academic skills, practicing the use of prompts to create the desired student behaviors, providing opportunities for the student to practice the behaviors, and the critically important step of delivering feedback to the student about any (even marginally incremental) behavioral improvements. Remember that if students are proficient in the desired behaviors, you should use this time to support their academic progress.

Despite the very best efforts of teachers at the first two tiers, there may be some evidence that indicates a student lacks the basic foundational skills required to demonstrate proficiency in desired behaviors. Behaviors at this level are generally unique to the student and may be harmful to him- or herself or to others. These students require Tier 3 supports (in addition to Tiers 1 and 2). The ABC analysis mentioned previously (page 66) may yield some important information at this tier.

The challenge that occurs at Tier 3 is finding the time to implement the necessary strategies. This essential work often needs to occur in place of other equally important content. Removing students from the general classroom should not be the first or only option, as it is important for students not reaching behavioral proficiency to be around students who are proficient. It makes little sense to take all of the ill-behaved students at a grade level and house them in their own isolated program. If the only behavior they witness is similarly inappropriate to theirs, how will they ever learn the appropriate, prosocial behavior? There will be occasions when some students, for their own safety or the safety of others, might benefit from some time in isolation from peers. However, this should not be the automatic option in lieu of high-quality, intentional instruction.

Evidence gathering is not part of a specific curriculum or program. Rather, it is a framework for promoting access to the highest quality core instruction. It is about formulating a plan to provide increasingly intensive interventions tailored to each student in a timely manner. It's not about waiting for the time and circumstances to be perfect, as perfect is the enemy of progress. It's not about blaming circumstance, shaming students, or blaming parents. It is about framing systematic measures of student progress that yield data for making critical education decisions.

Applying Differentiation Strategies for Behavior

As with any academic learning target, the key to all students becoming proficient in social behaviors (like cooperation, respect, or attentiveness) or academic behaviors (like metacognition, self-regulation, or motivation) is to have a plan to scaffold the learning and meet the needs of students at their current levels. Here are some suggestions for differentiation strategies that may be helpful.

- **Modify the learning environment:** With a proactive approach (if we can predict it, we can prevent it), teachers identify and modify specific environmental variables that may contribute to problem behavior. The classroom layout, agenda of activities, procedures and routines, and instructional strategies are all areas that teachers have under their control. Modifying these variables may preclude the classroom environment being a contributor to the problem behavior. Effective seating plans can support a variety of student interactions (such as small groups, partners, or whole class). Situating the desks of students exhibiting problem behaviors where there is less traffic or distraction and in closer proximity to the teacher and any required materials can be effective.

- **Decrease student uncertainty:** One of the areas that presents a significant challenge for students not yet proficient in desired behavior outcomes is during noninstructional or transition time. Teachers can prepare students for transitions by providing a warning about the close of one activity and the opening of another; giving clear and brief directions; planning for any materials needed and having them on hand; and starting the next content piece immediately. Teacher proximity to individual students during the directions will further minimize distractions.

- **Provide opportunities to make choices:** Student engagement increases and disruption decreases when students are offered choices. With careful consideration, teachers can create opportunities in their lessons that provide students options for how they participate. Consider the order or number of activities, the choice of materials to use, or if the student can work with a partner.

- **Identify positive ways for the student to communicate:** As an extension of giving students options, work with students on their ability to self-identify when they are on the verge of demonstrating some negative behavior. This could involve the color cards mentioned in chapter 5 (page 67) or an agreed-on time-out area of the room.

- **Adapt instruction:** Teachers should use a variety of instructional strategies and locations in the classroom to maximize student engagement. Placing high-interest activities after challenging learning targets (academic or behavioral) may serve as an incentive for students to work toward demonstrating proficiency.

- **Recognize positive behaviors:** When a student behaves appropriately, reinforce the behavior. Do not make this contingent on the behavior prior to the positive display. Students do recognize when they misbehave and may self-correct quickly by demonstrating the desired behavior. This is the moment to acknowledge their growth. It is also very important that the adults model the desired behavior. For example, if a student is being disrespectful and respect is the desired outcome, the adult must engage in his or her own next steps respectfully. Notice that I did not say the teacher should avoid consequences; it is important to attend to disrespectful behavior. However, a teacher is not going to effectively teach a student about respect if he or she instead reverts to disrespecting the student.

All these strategies require practice and some intention on the teachers' part to affect change. They need an approach that looks beyond the students' current status and does not hold grudges or blame the students' home environment. Barbara Coloroso is widely attributed as saying, in an unverified quote, "If kids come to us from strong, healthy, functioning families, it makes our job easier. If they do not come to us from strong, healthy, functioning families, it makes our job more important."

In chapter 1, I talked about the expectations teachers should have, and then distinguished setting expectation from the traditional approach of creating rules. As educators think about differentiation, it's important to reflect back on expectations and think about three steps to ensure they become part of the way the classroom operates.

1. Be clear on the expectations.

2. Plan for how to teach the expectations in an engaging and memorable fashion.

3. Think of a typical school year and when students might need a booster (reteach session). For some, the time needed may be as short as a long weekend. In general, any extended break may necessitate a review when students return.

The language of the expectations needs to become so familiar to students that they truly internalize that this is how the classroom will operate. The language of expectations should be clear through praise opportunities and efforts to remediate. Students need to connect to the expectations, and repetition will drive their work. Redundancy builds fluency in this matter.

Implementing Intervention Strategies for Students With Behavioral Gaps

In the previous section, I presented some differentiation strategies that may be helpful when determining the next steps in students gaining proficiency. When a student has challenges that are behavioral in nature, or the behavior is at the root of the academic struggle, some further interventions might be necessary. These intervention strategies will require additional time to implement and will need to be monitored for student progress.

Problem Solving to Address Behavioral Challenges

As a method to help students develop self-control and inner discipline, Coloroso (1994) suggests that teaching problem solving is a critical element. She outlines a six-step process for problem solving to address behavioral challenges.

Teachers could consider using this process with students until they internalize the steps and can practice the skills independently.

1. **Define the problem:** A critical first step in problem solving to address behavioral challenges is to define the problem. When students misbehave, too often it is seen as a motivational issue or a "won't do" problem. However, several misbehaviors are due to a lack of appropriate skills or a "can't do" challenge, not a lack of motivation. Defining the problem as a "can't do" challenge or a skill deficit leads to an approach of solving chronic misbehaviors through precorrection and skill building.

2. **Brainstorm solutions:** The act of brainstorming may take some time, and some students may need the opportunity to reflect and think about possible solutions. It is important, however, that the potential solutions come from the students.

3. **Evaluate the possible solutions against a set of criteria:** For this step, the role of the teacher is to help students evaluate their actions in terms of possible consequences. Coloroso (1994) suggests that the solutions should be evaluated using the criteria of whether or not the consequences of the possible solution are unfair, hurtful, unkind, or dishonest. Teachers may generate other criteria based on the situation.

4. **Select an option:** After the evaluations previously mentioned, students select the "best fit" option that addresses the misbehavior, allows for growth, and meets the needs of all participants, including the teacher.

5. **Plan the implementation:** With a potential solution, the implementation phase is key. It is important that this step be neither too complex nor prone to interfere with the positive learning environment of others. Gear the implementation to maximize success.

6. **Review the problem:** This step is a summary for students and a check for understanding for the teacher. It is a review of the previous five steps and an opportunity to plan to avoid a similar situation later.

Problem solving to address behavioral challenges in this manner will take time. Do not use these interventions for minor problems. Instead, utilize these strategies for more serious concerns that interfere with the learning environment of others.

Check-In Check-Out

Check-In Check-Out (CICO) is a research-based monitoring and mentoring tool that can support students as they build better habits, including self-monitoring behavior. Identify a CICO staff mentor (someone who has or is willing to have a relationship with the student). This adult and other involved staff will frequently monitor the student's behavior while he or she builds better habits. The eight steps of this process are as follows.

1. Establish times and procedures for checking in and checking out. These are the meeting times at the beginning and end of each day of the monitoring.

2. Note frequencies of CICO with relevant staff on a CICO form.

3. Explain the target behaviors and related focus strategies on a CICO form.

4. Have the student reflect on and rate his or her performance in relation to the target behaviors on the CICO form at the conclusion of each predetermined time period.

5. Ask the student to present the CICO form at the conclusion of each time period.

6. Rate the student's performance on the target behaviors. It is unnecessary to use staff members' time for conversation and debrief; the CICO mentor will guide reflection and debrief.

7. During check-out, determine daily point totals (based on successful demonstration of the desired behavior) and reinforce positive behaviors. It's also important to acknowledge growth.

8. Periodically (typically at the end of each week) plot daily point totals. The student and mentor reflect on progress and establish future goals.

Use CICO for students whose problem behaviors are unresponsive to Tier I interventions and who do not require more immediate individualized interventions. This strategy can provide both the steps to achieve a solution and, ultimately, the solution itself.

Behavior Education Program (BEP)

An extension of CICO, the behavior education program (BEP) is a system of support implemented for students who are not responding to core supports. The teacher, a parent, or other connected adult can refer students to the BEP if there is a need for increased behavior support. The BEP aims to prevent students from engaging in severe problem behavior. In the parlance of the positive behavior interventions and supports (PBIS) initiative, the BEP is about shrinking the yellow zone by helping students shift toward more green zone behavior and avoid drifting into red zone behavior (see figure 6.1).

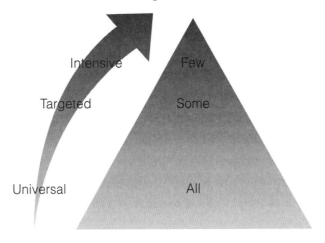

Figure 6.1: PBIS behavior pyramid.

*Visit **go.SolutionTree.com/behavior** for a free reproducible version of this figure.*

The need for a BEP could be evident by an increase in office discipline referrals, in-school suspensions, time out from class, or other tiered consequences for not meeting proficiency in the desired outcomes. Fortunately, it appears that the BEP is successful in reducing problem behaviors for a majority of student participants. Robert E. March and Robert H. Horner (2002) examine reducing rates of office discipline referrals with middle school students through the establishment of a BEP. They find that 67 percent of students who receive the BEP intervention have reductions in office discipline referrals following implementation. A similar study Leanne S. Hawken (2006) conducted finds that 75 percent of the middle school students who participate in the BEP have reductions in office discipline referrals. The effectiveness of the BEP lies in the early response, before behaviors get so entrenched that remediation becomes protracted. As students start to exhibit more yellow zone, off-task behavior, it's important that teachers intervene while the opportunity to connect back to the desired outcomes is still achievable. The evidence supports the notion that the BEP is a proactive strategy that will allow teachers to spend more time on maintaining a positive learning environment.

Case Study: A Pod Approach to Tier 3 Behavior

Schools today are faced with all of the historic challenges that a high-quality public education system engenders. In addition, some of the external levers that once provided a buffer to those challenges are no longer readily available. Specifically, when graduation rates are examined, we see a dichotomy emerge: while the nation's graduate rates are approaching all-time high levels, the lack of opportunity for those failing to graduate is also direr than ever before. This was previously less impactful when there were many more "living wage" jobs available for non-completers. The shift from a majority of jobs in the manufacturing and agricultural sectors to service-related fields has placed a higher premium on students graduating as well as completing further studies.

This speaks to the need for schools to pursue more aggressively the oft-stated mantra of "success for all" and to abandon any practices that deter from this goal. Chief among these is eliminating the practice of separating out students into regular education and special education. Rather than "sentencing" students to special education, schools should create authentic educational opportunities for all students that utilize the special skills of educators.

One school took the approach of identifying its ten most academically challenging students. These students also were very challenging in their behavior. As Austin Buffum, Mike Mattos, and Chris Weber (2009) point out, "Behavior and academic achievement are inextricably linked. A student's academic success in school is directly related to the student's attention, engagement, and behavior" (p. 111). Rather than proceeding with the traditional approach of creating a special program for these students (from which few ever emerge to return to the general program), the school clustered these students in two groups called pods and placed them in a class with an equal number of positive peer role models and "average" students. The school identified three desired intervention outcomes.

1. Utilize the strengths of the educators to effect positive change in struggling learners.

2. Better align human and financial resources to guide these outcomes.

3. Create a general education approach that encompassed the needs of all students.

The staff faced some initial concerns and obstacles.

- Which teachers would resist change to a model that removed "problem" students from regular classes?
- Who would teach these pod classes?
- What was the backup plan if this didn't work?
- What was the impact on the rest of the school?

One advantage to the proposal was that it required no extra time or resources; they simply integrated special education teachers, who previously worked with students in a separate room, into regular classrooms to offer targeted support. Teachers volunteered to teach these specially created classes and work with their newly embedded special education colleagues.

It was important to monitor this change and to have opportunity for feedback along the way. Teachers were aware of the high needs of these students, which were more pronounced on the behavior front. The commitment for the intervention was set for a fixed amount of time (a reporting term initially), and previous behavioral information on the students (office referrals and outcomes) served as a baseline for conversation on what was occurring.

The outcomes were largely positive and significant enough to dispel the notion of a return to the previous model of isolation. While the target students still had occasional struggles and outbursts, the frequency and severity decreased. Additionally, teachers noted more positive attributes than had previously been assigned to these students. As is the case with all students, even the most behaviorally challenged students had occasions where the content, instruction, and their personal motivation aligned, and these moments were positive for all. At a minimum, the school did not observe the situations in any classrooms getting worse or the behaviors becoming more severe than what they had been when these students were isolated.

If the expectation is that students displaying Tier 3 behavior will become adults that contribute positively to their communities, then schools must integrate these students in their school communities and immerse them in environments where they witness positive behaviors. Removing the label "severe behavior" that was previously attached to these students was a contributing factor to the positive gains. As Rice University researcher Dara Shifrer (2013) notes, "Teachers and parents are more likely to perceive disabilities in, and hold lower educational expectations for labeled adolescents than for similarly achieving and behaving adolescents not labeled with disabilities" (p. 462).

Teaching Gifted Students

One of the myths about gifted children is that they are all well-behaved, compliant students. In actuality, some get bored in class and may act out or call attention to the fact that they find class boring. Some whose social skills are less refined may ask inappropriate questions, call the teacher or other students dumb, or simply not play the "education game." They refuse to go through the motions of "doing school" and are not always compliant in their work output. Their needs are similar to other students experiencing a behavioral gap and their learning is just as critical. Some suggestions for the classroom teacher to consider include the following.

- **Teacher schedule:** It's important to give consideration to placing gifted and talented students with a teacher who enjoys teaching such a group and is willing to learn with and from them. Gifted and talented students don't need gifted and talented teachers as much as they need teachers who will challenge their limits and work with them to close the gaps.

- **Student schedule:** While keeping students of all abilities together is a positive outcome for classrooms, teachers should also consider providing regular opportunities for gifted and talented students to learn with and from their intellectual peers. This may involve creatively scheduling time with other classrooms or even other grade levels.

- **Engagement:** For all students, engagement has become a key element of schooling in the 21st century. Gifted and talented students need complex, challenging, and meaningful learning that causes them to stretch, as opposed to learning that validates or rehashes what they already know. Lack of engagement occasionally leads to a serious challenge and negative outcome—boredom.

- **Guidance:** Some gifted and talented students need to learn how to express their feelings and emotions. Teachers need to be prepared for this, rather than expecting the students' giftedness to be enough. I can recall an inappropriate response a student once gave when he was not experiencing any challenge in the class and was frustrated. He yelled out "Boring!" with as much gusto as he could muster. As inappropriate as it was, this outburst provided a great learning and teaching opportunity for all concerned. For the student, it was a lesson in learning to understand and cope with his giftedness in school (and later in society). For the teacher, it was a reminder that all students need to be stimulated while learning.

Gifted and talented students also need to be stretched in their school lives, both academically and behaviorally. As teachers continue to plan for the needs of *all* students in their classrooms, it's important to give this group the same opportunities for growth.

A Strategy to Consider

Educators need to be clear on learning targets and the end goal for each student. Clearly, if the learning target is writing proficiency, the student must be able to write. However, often educators default to requiring all assessments to be a pencil-and-paper output. Practices such as individual versus choral responses, written responses versus gestures, or peer-based assessment may be worth employing as educators differentiate to meet all students' needs.

Points Worth Remembering

- Differentiation works best when educators maximize the capacity of each student.
- Educators can differentiate on content, process, product, or environment.
- Enrichment is a form of differentiation that extends students' thinking, instead of just acknowledging it.
- Treffinger and Sortore (1992) state that enrichment has four levels: defining enrichment strategies for all, many, some, and few.
- Gathering evidence of proficiency is important—not to make excuses, but to make plans.
- Strategies that teachers might use as a response to evidence include RTI, RTI[2], MTSS, and CSSS.
- RTI and MTSS are important tools for managing challenging behavior and academics.

- Positive differentiation strategies for addressing challenging behavior include:
  - Modifying the learning environment
  - Decreasing student uncertainty
  - Providing opportunities to make choices
  - Identifying positive ways for students to communicate
  - Adapting instruction
  - Recognizing positive behaviors
- Coloroso (1994) provides six steps to assist in using problem solving to address challenging behaviors.
  a. Define the problem.
  b. Brainstorm solutions.
  c. Evaluate the possible solutions against a set of criteria.
  d. Select an option.
  e. Plan the implementation.
  f. Review the problem.
- CICO helps students build better habits.
- BEP is an extension of CICO and helps to address more severe behavior challenges.
- Gifted students may also have behavior deficiencies.

COLLABORATIVE TEAMS

Key 6: Collaborative Teams

Grade-level teachers (or cross-grade in small schools) engage in authentic collaboration during designated times to ensure positive expectations and outcomes for all students. A school-based team will receive a referral for a student when his or her misbehavior escalates or academics become a significant concern.

The thrust of this book thus far has been classroom specific, and that is still the intention. However, it is clear that teachers new to the profession or new to their roles or schools will benefit immensely from the connections they make with colleagues and the support they receive from those colleagues. With that as the backdrop, let's explore the many benefits of effective collaboration.

Collaboration

I began my teaching career in 1983 when the teaching profession was very much characterized by isolation (working individually behind closed doors). If there was something a teacher did that worked successfully, he or she kept it to himself or herself. There were often references to *my students* or *your students* when behavioral challenges emerged. When my daughter began her teaching career, I was excited to see that the modern teaching environment has become more collegial, driven by teachers' desires and motivations to work in a more connected fashion. Conversations about supportive interventions for students with behavior concerns are now about "our students."

Collaboration is an essential part of the work of teachers and is critical for those new to the profession or new to their schools. Kecia Dennis is a veteran middle school teacher in Richland Hills, Texas. She reflects on a key factor during her first year of teaching: "The first lifeline of my career came in the form of supportive colleagues. Having strong, helpful people to come alongside you and encourage you is the first resource to seek when walking into a classroom" (personal communication, June 3, 2014).

Some schools have a formalized mentorship program in place, and the benefits from such programs are significant. These programs often enhance the effects of a beginning teacher's initial preparation. Linda Darling-Hammond (2003) speaks to the benefits by suggesting, "Young teachers not only stay in the profession at higher rates but also become competent more quickly than those who must learn by trial and error" (p. 10). The significance of this collaboration extends beyond the impact on new teachers. Darling-Hammond (2003) further notes, "As an additional benefit, these programs provide a new lease on life for many veteran teachers. Veterans need ongoing challenges to remain stimulated and excited about the profession" (p. 12). While it's clearly desirable to have a mentoring structure in place, a lack of a formalized program should not be viewed as a reason to not engage in a more collaborative approach. As Hierck et al. (2011) note, "One of the most intelligent ways to perform our work is to share ideas, share the load, and share successes" (p. 82). First-year teacher Shannon Prosser speaks about the importance of collegial support:

> *In a more practical sense, a real challenge I feel is my lack of resources or unit plans for teaching the students what they need to know. In this era of education, textbooks and work sheets aren't cutting it anymore. We need to find new ways and mediums through which to teach our students. What I find incredibly helpful is having veteran teachers who are willing to take the time to mentor and share their ideas with new teachers. Teaching experience is what creates great teachers, not university programs. There is only so far our training will take us; the rest depends on the learning we do on the job and having other teachers share this valuable knowledge is definitely useful. (personal communication, December 28, 2015)*

Compliance Versus Commitment

Let's be clear, working in isolation can seem a lot easier than working in collaboration with others. If teachers are told they *have to* collaborate, it's less likely to be as effective as when they *want to* collaborate. The ease of working alone may seem preferable as teachers, feeling overwhelmed by the demands on their time, seek to retreat to their classroom to focus on "my students and my lessons." The unfortunate reality is that this, in effect, limits potential solutions to problems and causes undue stress and pressure on new teachers. I believe this is one of the reasons why some teachers leave the profession. While working alone is easier, it also means that challenges are processed alone, and this can be overwhelming. In my work with preservice teachers, working in isolation became the primary topic of the discussions we held after they completed their practicum teaching cycles. Hierck and Weber (2014a) state, "The reality is that the more educators inform their practice through the exchange of best practices, the work can become less stressful and feelings of professional isolation less debilitating" (p. 60).

Collaboration must be meaningful for teachers to realize its value. If collaboration merely degenerates to teachers gathering to confess the sins of our students and speaking about them in terms of their deficiencies, then not much benefit will be accrued. If, instead, the time is used to gather further strategies, talk about progress, plan next steps, and celebrate the gains achieved, collaboration can be a powerful tool. Having more heads thinking about solutions should yield more solutions. Collaboration is not universal agreement; rather, it is pushing each other to grow and learn more to achieve the desired student outcomes.

Once teachers realize the value of collaboration, all educators move toward the establishment of a collective commitment. Collaboration gets confused occasionally with universal agreement or all heads nodding in unison. That's not collaboration and often reflects resignation—that it's better to agree and be left alone than to challenge and be chastised. Additionally, universal agreement can often indicate redundancy—if four people agree on everything then three might not participate in the dialogue. Healthy collaboration exists when there is respectful disagreement and some form of cognitive dissonance. Collaboration that aims to produce a collective commitment should focus on "teaching and learning and should not be wasted on less-professionally oriented tasks or simply on identifying problems for others to solve" (Hierck & Weber, 2014a, p. 60).

It can be a challenge (especially when a teacher is new) to tell the difference between compliance and commitment. How do teachers really know that their colleagues are operating with a sense of collective commitment and not simply choosing an easier road by being in-the-moment compliant? Williams and Hierck (2015) suggest these indicators of collective commitment:

- *As part of the collaborative team, you're either getting better at your job or helping someone else get better.*

- *There are no excuses, just variables. Your teams focus on what you can control instead of what you can't, that is, outside factors such as issues at home, parental support, socioeconomic challenges, and language.*

- *You and everyone on your staff understand that every child is "your" child, and the failure of any one of them is not an option. (pp. 53–54)*

Teams

A collaborative team consists of a group of individuals who share common beliefs and a desire to work toward common goals. Collaborative teams discuss what they hope to accomplish and set team and individual goals for reaching their collective commitment. Team members have varying areas of expertise and share tasks, resources, responsibilities, and leadership. They don't always agree on everything and stretch each other's thinking to achieve a greater solution together than might have been achieved apart. Richard DuFour, Rebecca DuFour, Robert Eaker, Thomas M. Many, and Mike Mattos (2016) provide an action-oriented structure for collaborative teams in professional learning communities that focuses the response of educators to four critical questions.

1. What is it we want all students to learn?

2. How will we know when each student has mastered the essential learning?

3. How will we respond when a student experiences initial difficulty in learning?

4. How will we deepen the learning for students who have already mastered essential knowledge and skills?

Hierck and Weber (2014b), in their book *RTI Roadmap for School Leaders*, extend these four questions to examine those students who have not yet attained proficiency at the universal instruction level (Tier 1):

1. About which students do we have concerns?

2. Why are students experiencing difficulties: academics, academic behaviors, or social behaviors?

3. What are we currently doing to support the student and meet the student's needs? What supports will we be providing in the future?

4. To what extent have students responded to instruction and intervention?

Regardless of the questions that drive collaborative teams, it is teachers working productively with their colleagues to serve students that drive the next steps.

It is intuitive that collaborative teams will look different with each school or situation new teachers find themselves in, and they will need to adjust to that local context. Teachers in small schools who are the only teacher at that grade or content level often ask me how collaborative teams might work for their situation. Some options available include vertical teams (working across grade levels in the same content domain), similar content teams (where the content areas overlap—for example, in graphing or persuasive writing), teachers in nearby schools or communities (setting up regular dialogue and meeting time is key) or technology-assisted teams (Twitter or Google Hangouts are two of my favorite ways to communicate at a distance). Ultimately, it's not important that collaborative teams consist of individuals doing exactly the same task or facing exactly the same problems. Rather, teams should include teachers who share a common interest and effort. This shared goal will ensure that the focus of the team remains on the right work and will support educators as they build their capacity to work together.

Data Teams

Data teams clarify the school's data vision and model the use of data to support instructional decision making. This team engages in collaborative decision making and makes available the evidence gathered for all teachers. The team can include administrators, teachers, classroom support professionals, and potentially district personnel to ensure the data team comprises representatives from different roles. Data teams should follow a five-step process to examine student work, apply effective instructional strategies (including interventions), and monitor student learning in response to those strategies and interventions (see figure 7.1, page 96).

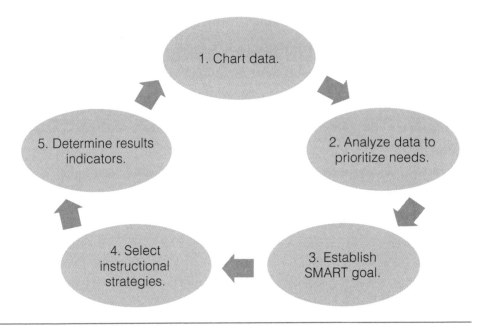

Figure 7.1: Five-step process for data teams.

*Visit **go.SolutionTree.com/behavior** for a free reproducible version of this figure.*

This model aligns very effectively with the steps identified in RTI in chapter 6 (page 77). Tier 1 calls for high-quality, differentiated instruction in academics and behavior for all students. To meet this goal, teachers should collaboratively examine evidence of student response to academic and behavioral instructional strategies. When a student does not respond to this focused, differentiated, universal instruction, teachers must supplement their instruction with Tier 2 supports, regardless of the needs being academic or behavioral or both. This could mean more time, the use of alternative strategies, more frequency, smaller adult-to-student ratios, or more targeted interventions. The data collected and the collaborative planning and analysis by the team defines the next steps plan. The student's response to the targeted intervention should be why a team decides to increase the intensity of these additional Tier 2 supports. As outlined previously, providing Tiers 2 and 3 supports *in addition to* the universal Tier 1 instruction is essential. These additional, supplemental interventions serve to augment core instruction, not supplant it.

Cautions for Collaboration

Collaboration must be effectively planned out and the time utilized in pursuit of agreed-upon outcomes. The first of these requirements is the easier of the two to achieve, and I've worked in many schools where collaborative time is built into the weekly schedule. However, merely providing the time does not make it effective. In a toxic school culture, teachers are more likely to use the time provided for collaboration to reinforce their negative views of students, parents, or colleagues. Excuse making typically dominates the agenda and the meeting time deteriorates into complaint sessions. Making collaboration time effective begins with building a culture that believes in the potential of all students and has all teachers striving toward that outcome.

Collaboration Without a Purpose

Collaboration can be ineffective if the participants involved lack a defined and clearly stated purpose. Michael Fullan and Joanne Quinn (2016) offer this cautionary note: "Collaboration as an end in itself is a waste of time. Groups are powerful, which means that they can be powerfully wrong. Getting deeper without the discipline and specificity of collective deliberation can be a grand waste of time" (p. 13). They claim that achieving coherence comes with the pursuit of the right objectives for the right reasons and emphasize the need to focus direction, cultivate collaborative cultures, deepen learning, and secure accountability (Fullan & Quinn, 2016). The success of collaboration, then, all connects back to its purpose—the *why* of the work.

Ineffective Collaboration With Parents

Ineffective communication between parents and teachers can be a major obstacle when teachers are trying to solve problems with students. Parents fulfill many roles as their children begin school, grow, and transition from elementary to middle to high school, and to their lives beyond. Supporting the parents' roles of decision maker, team member, and teacher greatly enhances the ability of the classroom teacher to develop a personalized intervention that has the greatest potential to help the student gain proficiency. While the input of parents is mandated by federal statutes such as the Individuals With Disabilities Education Act (IDEA; 2004), which states that a parent must be an active member of the Individualized Education Program (IEP) team and that the creation of an IEP should result from the efforts of both the parents and the school district, this should not be the sole reason for engaging parents. Trying to educate students without the support and advice of their parents is like raking leaves in a high wind; it may seem like progress until you turn around and see the pile once again dispersed.

When parents and teachers collaborate to form a team, they ensure that the student receives individualized assessment, evaluation, and intervention. Parents participate as members of the assessment team, provide information for the IEP, and provide input on the evaluation of the progress the student makes toward meeting the identified goals. Parents also provide information and act as contributors in understanding the needs and motivations of the student on a day-to-day basis, as this will guide the actions of teachers. Parents know how their child will act within the context of their family, community, and culture. They can share insights not always visible at school, including how the student organizes and solves problems, what he or she fears, and his or her coping strategies or emotional hot button issues. Here are some collaboration strategies teachers might consider when talking with parents.

- Focus on the problem, not the people involved. The interventions the teacher suggests should be about changing the behavior, not the student.

- Be open to new ideas.

- Ask clarifying questions.

- Find common ground.

- Don't force a solution.

- Pick solutions that both the teacher and the parent agree on.

- Plan and agree on the next steps.

I am aware that some readers will be frustrated as their attempts to draw parents in are sometimes met with resistance. What can teachers do with a parent who is unavailable, unresponsive, or unwilling to acknowledge a problem (let alone work to solve the problem)? The short answer is, keep trying! I have seen schools where food has worked. For example, one school introduced the new mathematics curriculum by hosting a "Noodles and Numbers" evening. Working parents often appreciate having dinner provided at the end of a long day, so this was a win for them. The win for the school was an audience of parents who got to hear about the new mathematics curriculum. I also knew when I became a school leader that it was important for me to talk to parents and discern why they had not been to school or responded to our messages. This is important for teachers, and often enlightening. For some, the rationale harkened back to their own school experience, which was negative and still residing within their memories. When it comes to behavior, the best time to try and engage a parent is when the problem first occurs and the solution is relatively simple. Calling a parent the first time a student forgets his or her pen and asking for support is easier to resolve than calling a parent after the fifth time the student forgets the pen and trying to justify the consequence about to be imposed. Parents are an integral part of the team supporting the progress of each student, so teachers will need to consider going above and beyond for those parents not yet engaged in the process.

Student Collaboration and Social and Emotional Learning

Educators routinely accept that student proficiency in reading, writing, and mathematics influences their ability to succeed later. As a result, much is made of the need to structure academic opportunities, to increase rigor, and to teach and assess at the creating and evaluating levels further up Bloom's taxonomy. However, researchers Frances Anne Freitas and Lora J. Leonard (2011) indicate that more time spent on Maslow's hierarchy could yield equally significant benefits in student proficiency. As a result, teachers should plan to spend more time on student-to-student collaborative areas like sharing, problem solving, and cooperating to build students' social and emotional learning (SEL) and close some proficiency gaps. This aligns well with the lower levels of Maslow's hierarchy (see figure 3.1, page 36), including the levels referring to physiological needs and safety and security needs. Building this base will allow students to gain the confidence necessary to take the next steps in their learning progression.

Social and emotional learning describes the process and delineates the actions teachers can use to help students acquire the knowledge, attitudes, and skills to understand their emotions, set goals, learn empathy for others, maintain positive relationships, and make responsible decisions. Teachers should incorporate SEL into daily Tier 1 instruction as they engage students in positive activities. Some SEL programs teach social and emotional skills directly, like those relating to substance abuse prevention, violence prevention, health promotion, and character education, while others have instructional components that foster safe, caring, engaging, and participatory learning environments that help students build connections to school and their motivation to learn. The Collaborative for Academic, Social, and Emotional Learning (CASEL; 2003) identifies five key competencies that teachers should teach, practice, and reinforce through SEL instructional design.

1. Self-awareness is the ability to recognize one's own emotions, interests, strengths, and limitations.

2. Self-management refers to the ability to regulate one's own emotions and manage daily stressors.

3. Social awareness refers to the capacity to take others' perspectives and to appreciate similarities and differences.

4. Relationship skills are when individuals exhibit prosocial behavior and demonstrate positive social skills in order to develop meaningful relationships.

5. Responsible decision making refers to the capacity to make ethical decisions and develop appropriate solutions to identified problems.

These five key competencies are important throughout life but are especially impactful as children enter school and begin to socialize with peers. They also affect whether students are able to engage fully in learning and whether they benefit from instruction.

Research indicates that social competency is a strong predictor of future success (Jones, Greenberg, & Crowley, 2015). Results from a longitudinal study by researchers from Pennsylvania State and Duke universities that analyzed outcomes of SEL on nearly eight hundred kindergarteners provide very compelling data in support of this point. Teachers measured social competency skills when the subjects were in kindergarten. Students received scores on a range of social behaviors, such as whether they can resolve peer problems, listen to others, share materials, cooperate, and display helpfulness. Each student received a composite score representing his or her overall level of positive social skills and behavior on a scale from zero (not at all) to four (very well). Researchers then monitored the students for the positive and negative milestones they accomplished until they reached the age of twenty-five. The study found that for every one-point increase in a student's social competence score in kindergarten, he or she is:

◆ Fifty-four percent more likely to earn a high school diploma

◆ Twice as likely to attain a college degree in early adulthood

◆ Forty-six percent more likely to have a full-time job at the age of twenty-five

For every one-point decrease in a student's social competence score in kindergarten, he or she has a:

- Sixty-four percent higher chance of spending time in juvenile detention

- Sixty-seven percent higher chance of being arrested by early adulthood

- Fifty-two percent higher rate of recent binge drinking and 82 percent higher rate of recent marijuana usage

- Eighty-two percent higher chance of being in or on a waiting list for public housing

Jennifer Ng'andu, Olga Acosta Price, and Wendy Baron (2015) suggest that students can learn social skills and that the earlier teachers commit to teaching these skills, the better the outcomes. These researchers highlight six simple strategies from the New Teacher Center for teachers to put into practice while promoting academic learning.

1. **Help students know themselves:** "Classroom routines like 'morning circle' or 'connections and reflections' offer a safe setting in which students learn to name their feelings and identify their strengths and challenges" (Ng'andu et al., 2015).

2. **Have students stand in others' shoes:** "The crucial thinking skill of taking other perspectives supports academic success along with social competence" (Ng'andu et al., 2015). Students can practice empathy through games, role playing, or debates.

3. **Teach students to seek and give feedback:** "Being receptive to useful feedback sets children up for lifelong learning. Even younger students can look at exemplars of excellence, and see how their own work could improve" (Ng'andu et al., 2015). Recall Nuthall's (2007) analysis that reveals 80 percent of the feedback a student receives is from peers and that 80 percent of this feedback is incorrect. Students' ability to both deliver and receive feedback is a critical skill to be developed.

4. **Practice listening:** "Young people think more deeply and communicate more clearly when we explicitly teach, practice, and assess listening skills" (Ng'andu et al., 2015). Students may be tuning out, jumping to conclusions, interrupting, or dismissing ideas because they have not learned the requisite skill of listening. Remind students that we have

two ears and one mouth and should use those proportionally. As an added bonus, teachers who listen know more about their students!

5. **Teach collaboration:** "Those who start to work with others early will use those skills throughout their academic, work, and personal lives. When we regularly model, practice, and assess collaboration, children learn to share the mic, make plans with others, take on a role, and come to solutions together" (Ng'andu et al., 2015). Ensure that groups are not static but rather flow, so all students eventually work together. This will validate collaboration as essential learning.

6. **Treat mistakes as opportunities:** "In the old days, perfection got the praise. Then neuroscience showed us that we learn more by risking a mistake. Teachers can instill this mindset early by treating every mistake as an opportunity" and modeling this in their personal practice (Ng'andu et al., 2015). This mindset develops "curious, creative, and motivated learners who will thrive and contribute, regardless of what their futures hold" (Ng'andu et al., 2015). Often, if students are afraid to make mistakes, there is little growth because students play it safe.

The myriad of issues facing today's educators and students is daunting and seemingly ever growing. School staff must routinely step in as new challenges emerge in communities—and even more is expected from employers and post-secondary institutions. The solutions will not emerge from solely concentrating on improving academic scores on external exams, as Joseph E. Zins and Maurice J. Elias (2006) suggest:

> *Genuinely effective schools—those that prepare students not only to pass tests at school but also to pass the tests of life—are finding that social–emotional competence and academic achievement are interwoven and that integrated, coordinated instruction in both areas maximizes students' potential to succeed in school and throughout their lives. (p. 1)*

The National Center for Education Statistics (2001) states that among the major reasons cited for dropping out of school, several involve social and emotional factors: not getting along with teachers (35.0 percent) or peers (20.1 percent), feeling left out (23.2 percent), and not feeling safe (12.1 percent). Building social and emotional skills in students from an early age through collaborative activities will mitigate the impact of these factors and work toward more students making successful transitions throughout the education system.

A Strategy to Consider

When asking students to engage in peer evaluation, guiding language is helpful as they collaborate. Greg Wolcott, an assistant superintendent for teaching and learning in Woodridge, Illinois, has created the GAS card (glow, ask, and shine) that offers students the opportunity to provide constructive feedback through the use of guides and prompts (see table 7.1). This tool teaches students how to give and receive appropriate feedback that will allow them to reflect on their learning and plan for next steps.

Table 7.1: Sample GAS Card for Student Feedback

Glow	Give your partner a glow by recognizing something specific that helped you understand his or her work.	When you _____, it helped me understand _____ because _____. I thought _____ was effective because _____. I could connect with _____ because _____.
Ask	Ask a question about the topic to assist your partner in self-identifying the next steps on his or her personal learning path.	What made you decide to _____? Could you clarify what you meant by _____? What did you mean when you said _____? What would happen if _____?
Shine	Help your partner's work shine brighter by working together to make it better. Make a suggestion for improvement.	Next time I think you could try _____ because _____. Instead of _____ how about _____ because _____. A suggestion I would make for next time would be to _____ because _____.

Source: G. Wolcott, personal communication, March 8, 2016.
*Visit **go.SolutionTree.com/behavior** for a free reproducible version of this table.*

Points Worth Remembering

- New and old teachers will benefit immensely from the connections they make with colleagues and the support they receive from those colleagues. Collaboration means shifting the conversation from *my* students to *our* students.
- Mentor teachers play a significant role for new or new-to-the-school teachers.
- Compliance produces minimal growth; collective commitment makes all educators better.
- Collaborative teams achieve a greater solution together than could be achieved apart. They don't always agree but they always agree to collaborate.
- A data team is an example of a collaborative team that guides educators through effective data dialogue.
- Fullan and Quinn (2016) caution that collaborating without a purpose can be ineffective.
- Parents are important members of the collaborative team.
- Build social and emotional learning (SEL) on these five key competencies.
    - a. Self-awareness
    - b. Self-management
    - c. Social awareness
    - d. Relationship skills
    - e. Responsible decision making
- There is a direct correlation between social competency and school success. A lack of social competency results in antisocial adult behaviors.
- Ng'andu et al. (2015) identify six strategies educators can use to teach social skills.
    - a. Help students know themselves.
    - b. Have students walk in the shoes of others.
    - c. Teach students to seek and give feedback.
    - d. Practice listening.
    - e. Teach collaboration.
    - f. Treat mistakes as opportunities.

CONNECTION TO THE SCHOOLWIDE SYSTEM

Key 7: Connection to the Schoolwide System

Systems are in place to ensure that all other keys align with school-wide expectations. The systems are secure enough to withstand staff changes, yet flexible enough to accommodate changes in situations and circumstances as they arise.

The previous chapters have covered a lot of ground and presented many opportunities for teachers to create positive learning environments in their classrooms. Here is what we have examined thus far.

- ◆ Teachers should set and support high expectations for student behavior and articulate a focused set of common expectations.

- ◆ Teachers should deliver targeted instruction to all students.

- ◆ Teachers should positively reinforce and recognize appropriate behaviors when displayed by students.

- ◆ Teachers should use data as evidence for adjusting, modifying, or reteaching specific skills. The focus is on learning, not earning.

- ◆ Teachers should instill collaborative and creative ways of supporting and intervening with students as their needs indicate and as the tiers of support provide.

- ◆ Schools and districts should put collaborative practices in place to support new teachers and to provide opportunities to engage in data-driven dialogue. Collaborative practices will also support individual students at risk of behavioral issues.

Despite this background, one critical component is still missing: that connective piece that aligns all of the classrooms in a school—not in a lock-step, one-size-fits-all approach, but in a cohesive, collective, supportive approach that speaks to a team. School faculties will not become teams if the staff continue to work in silos. A team develops from a group that clearly understands its collective commitment and does not devolve to pockets of excellence. In other words, the work extends beyond the collaborative team of a grade, department, or content area to the work being embraced, modeled, and lived in the classrooms of every teacher in the school.

This key speaks to the need for teachers to have confidence in, and be confident for, their colleagues. When the expectations of each classroom are clearly aligned with the expectations of the entire school, the language for all of the educators is common and students more readily become fluent in that language. Remember, redundancy builds fluency. The more the expectations are consistently expected and understood, the greater the likelihood of them becoming commonplace. Think back to those students who challenge you the most. Those students need consistency from the adults in order to acquire and develop new habits. A University College of London study in 2009 asks the question, "How long does it take to form a habit?" (Lally et al., 2010, p. 998.) The results suggest that it takes an average of 66 days (the full range was 18 to 254 days, but 66 represented a sweet spot), with easier behaviors taking fewer days and tougher ones taking longer. If the expectations differ from classroom to classroom (or even by department or grade level) or from the classroom to the whole school, this challenge becomes almost impossible to overcome. Schoolwide expectations address the need for a consistent approach on what is delivered but not necessarily on how these are delivered.

It is tempting and may even seem logical to determine that the best way to limit external—and potentially harmful—influences on the classroom is to simply focus on what happens within the four classroom walls rather than the four broader walls of the entire school. Collaboration is messy and takes time. Teachers responding to their own individual needs and controlling their own individual domain seems infinitely easier and cleaner. This is an understandable mindset, and I firmly believe that every school is chock full of highly educated, well-intentioned, optimistic, hard-working, and dedicated staff who share this belief. However, individual, classroom-based approaches to behavioral interventions have their downsides—namely, a lack of consistency from year to year in student discipline, a lack of consistent expectations for students, and a lack of conversation around successful methods that have worked in other classrooms, for example.

In the absence of an agreed-on, universal approach to supporting all students as they learn and grow, there may still be the potential for random acts of improvement which result in pockets of excellence, as Kenneth C. Williams and Tom Hierck (2015) suggest:

> These schools have no real collective commitment to engage in high-leverage, research-based best practices and risk the quality of the student learning experience because that experience will depend entirely on which teacher the student gets. We find that many schools tolerate pockets of excellence. Why is it acceptable for one team to implement practices that you know are best for students, while you allow another team to opt out? Why resign yourself to wide variation in commitment to agreed-on best practices? (p. 60)

The best way to provide consistent, dependable behavioral interventions for students is for schools and districts to create schoolwide expectations and systems that can be effectively implemented in each classroom. The schools that do this are special because they make an overt commitment to working collaboratively, holding high expectations for students and themselves, and exhibiting the power of persistence. When teachers at such schools implement interventions or instructional strategies in their classrooms, at least one attribute must be non-negotiable: the efforts must be systematic. This is simply good practice and minimizes the potential arbitrariness of a school when educators can plan for success together, enact that plan, and see the benefits of changed student behavior as a result.

Systematic, Schoolwide Interventions

The impact of a universal approach that has its genesis in the classroom and is then supported across all classrooms is significant. Sometimes the struggle originates with knowing where to begin. Two strategies that have had success are the three-step process and the self-determination theory.

Three-Step Process

One example of a practice that is effective when systematically implemented in schools is the three-step process. In chapter 4, we examined direct to correct to connect approaches (page 47). Teachers might consider extending this approach to a three-step process to assist in managing classroom behaviors that are not in line with expectations. As with every strategy in this book, it's important to keep the context of the classroom, the needs of individual students, and the teacher's personal style in mind when defining the three steps. Here's an example of how to implement the three-step process from one of the schools I had the opportunity to work with.

1. **The teacher issues a verbal reminder to the student, connecting it to the desired expectation:** "Tommy, I need you to remain focused on the speaker as one of our ways to indicate respect." Note that the teacher does not stop with the lesson, but simply issues the verbal warning.

2. **The teacher writes the student's name on the board:** This is now a visual reminder to change a behavior in order for the respectful, positive learning environment to continue. This can also take the form of a stoplight system, movement of a clip, or personalized desktop mechanism. The point is to add another level or indicator so the student is clear that either a modification must occur or he or she must relay some indicator of difficulty in meeting expectations.

3. **The teacher asks the student to gather his or her materials and then escorts the student across the hall to a colleague's classroom:** This move serves as a reminder of the connection to respect for the student. All teachers agree to have an extra desk at the back of each classroom to accommodate a student who was unable to focus on the task that day.

The expectations for the receiving teachers should be clear; they do not have to start their own three-step process. The student may be sent to the office if he or she continues to misbehave. The administration, familiar with the three-step process, is then able to issue appropriate consequences and set up a learning opportunity for the student.

The impact of the three-step process is contingent on it being an understood expectation carried out by all teachers across the school. Don Mrozik is the principal of Sipley Elementary School in Woodridge, Illinois. He shares some thoughts on the impact of a schoolwide approach to the three-step process:

> *In many respects, the three-step process serves as a communicative device between teacher and student. Established expectations for behavior that promote a positive learning environment make clear*

what is needed for the highest levels of teaching and learning to occur
in a classroom. Based on those expectations, students are held account-
able for their choices in hopes that with feedback, students can adjust
behaviors that align with established expectations. (personal commu-
nication, December 30, 2015)

It's equally important that both the adults and the students understand that every day represents a fresh start. There is no carryover from the previous day regardless of whether a student moved to step two on the previous day. The impact of this process, and the long-term benefits that Mrozik refers to in the quote above, are realized when the expectations are rational and clear and steps consistently provide feedback to students when they move forward. The benefits are unrelated to which classroom or teacher a student is assigned to, but are instead driven by a common understanding of the expectations and the consequences and an adherence by the adults to making the system work schoolwide.

Self-Determination Theory

What if every teacher operated his or her classroom with the belief that students need not to be controlled but rather nurtured? Further, what if they could count on their colleagues to embrace a similar approach? These may represent two of the hardest *break-from* assumptions in schools today—the fear of losing control of the students and the chaos that ensues. Ed L. Deci and Richard M. Ryan (2000), pioneers of the self-determination theory, offer an alternative way of treating students that meshes with this line of thinking. Their research highlights the idea that individuals want to learn and will cooperate when they are in an environment that meets their basic needs. Deci and Ryan (2000) list four factors that students require to learn: (1) positive and nurturing relationships, (2) choice and autonomy, (3) a purpose for learning, and (4) a sense of progress from their efforts. Meeting these four conditions ensures individuals learn more deeply, value what they learn, and are interested in learning more. External rewards or incentives are neutral (they have neither a positive nor a negative impact on the outcome), as educators shift from the worry of *controlling* student behavior to the excitement of *influencing* it.

According to self-determination theory, educators should guide, coach, and facilitate rather than control or manipulate student behavior (Deci & Ryan, 2000). Instead of rushing to consequences, teachers should focus on the cause of the behavior. Table 8.1 (page 110) outlines some of the benefits of focusing on the causes of behavior by contrasting these with the negatives associated with the rush to consequences for the same behavior. As teachers continue to build the positive learning environment classroom by classroom, it is easy to see how an entire school or district could fully embrace this model. Once the focus is on understanding the cause of student behavior, the effect adult actions can have becomes clearer.

Table 8.1: Analysis of Consequences and Causation

Administering Consequences	Discovering Causes
Stops the behavior quickly; seeks immediate relief	Slowly stops behavior; delays relief
Teaches what not to do (direct)	Teaches what to do (connect)
Decreases self-concept or belief that "I am bad"	Increases the self-concept or belief that "my behavior is bad; I am not bad"
Decreases positive attitudes toward school and schoolwork	Increases positive attitudes toward school and schoolwork
Causes withdrawal (task completion, tardiness, truancy, dropping out)	Promotes enhanced participation and closing of behavioral gaps
Causes aggression (against property and others)	Decreases likelihood of aggression
Teaches students to respond in a punitive and angry manner	Teaches students to recognize the positive learning in each situation
Actions can harm or destroy student-teacher relationship	Actions can enhance student-teacher relationship

Visit **go.SolutionTree.com/behavior** *for a free reproducible version of this figure.*

True to Yourself

This might seem like an odd section in a chapter that speaks to connecting a teacher's individual practice to the practice of his or her colleagues and, by extension, to a whole-school approach. However, collaboration within a schoolwide system cannot sacrifice what an individual teacher knows works best for his or her students. In other words, I don't want best practice (not to be confused with the practice a teacher is best at) to be subsumed by being a team player. Many new teachers or teachers new to a school have shared their anxiety around trying to fit in and not wanting to get off on the wrong foot. This is that moment of being true to oneself. Is the teacher willing to remain principled in what he or she believes works best for students in this moment, even if it means standing alone? Can the teacher find the courage to respectfully disagree and present a rationale supporting what he or she does? Remember, being collaborative is not about always agreeing; it's about rallying the team behind what will produce the best outcomes.

Teachers have an unmatched capacity to influence others. They use it every day in their classrooms, at parent meetings, and in the community. Perseverance in the pursuit of what makes a difference for students is the right path for all educators, and teachers should strive to always follow that path. As teachers work to become part of the team at their schools—part of the collective commitment needed to ensure all students achieve the bar or better—they must not lose sight of the person they described in the interview that landed them the job. That's the person who's poised and able to make a difference for all students.

 ## A Strategy to Consider

PBIS expert Tim Lewis's (2007) environmental inventory (shared at the "Making Connections" conference) asks educators to score various components within their classrooms on a scale of 1 to 5. Administrators may use the modified inventory in figure 8.1 to delineate some key components that should be common across all classrooms in a school.

Rate each feature using a scale of 1 (inconsistent or unpredictable) to 5 (consistent and predictable).	
Behavior Management: Does the teacher have universal systems of PBIS in place?	
• Posts expectations	1 2 3 4 5
• Appropriately refers to expectations	1 2 3 4 5
• Gives students verbal praise for following expectations	1 2 3 4 5
• Makes corrections restating the expectation and stating the appropriate replacement behavior	1 2 3 4 5

Figure 8.1: Environmental inventory.   continued →

*Visit **go.SolutionTree.com/behavior** for a free reproducible version of this figure.*

• Uses a continuum of consequences for encouraging expected behaviors	1 2 3 4 5
• Maintains a four to one ratio of positive to negative statements	1 2 3 4 5
Routines: Does the teacher have procedures and routines that are clear and consistently followed?	
• For starting the class	1 2 3 4 5
• For working in groups	1 2 3 4 5
• For working independently	1 2 3 4 5
• For special events (movies, assemblies, snack time, parties)	1 2 3 4 5
• For obtaining materials and supplies	1 2 3 4 5
• For using equipment (for example, computers or tape players)	1 2 3 4 5
• For entering and exiting the classroom (using the restroom or drinking fountain, going to the library, moving around the room, and so on)	1 2 3 4 5

Source: Adapted from Lewis, 2007.

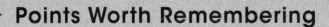

Points Worth Remembering

- Classroom interventions, systematically implemented in a collaborative intervention across schools or districts, will be most successful.
- The three-step process effectively extends the benefits of the direct to correct to connect continuum to the greater school environment.
- Teachers should nurture students, not attempt to control them.
- Deci and Ryan (2000) state that self-determination may be instilled in students through the following conditions.
    - Positive and nurturing relationships
    - Choice and autonomy
    - A purpose for learning
    - A sense of progress from their efforts

- The rush to consequences produces negative outcomes. Determining the cause (and addressing it) produces positive benefits.
- Persevere with best practice for the students even when others don't agree.

EPILOGUE

I'm a pretty positive person by nature. I wish I could say I've always behaved that way. Unfortunately, I've allowed myself to be negative and to not always give my best as an educator during my career, and those were the wrong choices to make. The role of the educator is about choice and about intentionally committing to making the right choice far more often than the wrong one. In doing that, I've discovered that the infrequent wrong choice is now easily forgiven and quickly forgotten.

When I read Viktor Frankl's (2006) book *Man's Search for Meaning*, I was amazed at how someone who not only survived the atrocities he experienced but emerged with such compassion and caring for his fellow humans. He came to realize that the final gift we all possess, that we cannot give up willingly, is the capacity to choose our response: "Everything can be taken from a man but one thing: the last of the human freedoms—to choose one's attitude in any given set of circumstances, to choose one's own way" (p. 104).

Thankfully, our work in schools only periodically encounters gut-wrenching events and situations. Most often, teachers have willing learners, willing adults, supportive families, and great communities. Why then, do some schools still struggle with results that lead to limited choices for students when they leave us? With graduation rates that in our largest cities barely hit the majority of the student population? With disparate results for those students who need teachers the most, who present the least fluency in the skills required for successful transition to the adult world, and who get defined more by the disaggregated label attached to them than by their capacity as learners? As I ponder these questions, I go back to the comments of teacher and psychologist Haim G. Ginott (1972):

> I've come to the frightening conclusion that I am the decisive element
> in the classroom. It's my personal approach that creates the climate.
> It's my daily mood that makes the weather. As a teacher, I possess a

115

tremendous power to make a child's life miserable or joyous. I can be a tool of torture or an instrument of inspiration. I can humiliate or humor, hurt or heal. In all situations, it is my response that decides whether a crisis will be escalated or de-escalated and a child humanized or dehumanized. (pp. 15–16)

This book offers a choice that all educators can make—to be intentionally and explicitly positive, to ensure quality relationships for all students, and to be the difference makers every educator sets out to be when he or she enters the profession. My reflections on the moments of my career when I was negative do not leave me with a sense of pride, nor do they allow me to hide behind the convenient excuse of what the students were doing. Rather, they resulted in some deep introspection and the decision to exercise a better option: to be intentionally positive. The choice to be positive by design does not demand perfection. It demands intention with an eye toward improving the life chances of every student. Being positive by design reflects the choice every educator gets to make daily, and the joy of this work lies not in predicting the future but in creating it.

Veteran teacher Elise Nicoletti sums up the role of the teacher and the hope I have for all educators when they reflect on their work:

I would not trade one moment of it for any other profession, because it was what I was called to do with my life. I am still discovering the meaning of each day as each moment unfolds in the classroom. The legacy I leave is yet to be determined, yet in the end, I hope to finally hear the words, "Well done, my good and faithful servant," because in the end, to have done the job well is all I really ever hoped to achieve. (personal communication, February 10, 2015)

So, colleague, what will your legacy be? Will you strive to leave a positive impact on every student you have the good fortune to teach? Will you add something to each one of them during the ten months they are in your care? Parents trust us with their most precious gift. Let's reward that trust and arm every student with the capacity to make a difference as they tackle the world beyond school.

REFERENCES AND RESOURCES

Battistich, V., & Hom, A. (1997). The relationship between students' sense of their school as a community and their involvement in problem behaviors. *American Journal of Public Health*, *87*(12), 1997–2001.

Becker, W. C., Engelmann, S., & Thomas, D. R. (1975). *Teaching 2: Cognitive learning and instruction*. Chicago: Science Research Associates.

Blackwell, L. S., Trzesniewski, K. H., & Dweck, C. S. (2007). Implicit theories of intelligence predict achievement across an adolescent transition: A longitudinal study and an intervention. *Child Development*, *78*(1), 246–263.

Buffum, A., Mattos, M., & Weber, C. (2009). *Pyramid response to intervention: RTI, professional learning communities, and how to respond when kids don't learn*. Bloomington, IN: Solution Tree Press.

Buffum, A., Mattos, M., & Weber, C. (2010). The why behind RTI. *Educational Leadership*, *68*(2), 10–16.

Collaborative for Academic, Social, and Emotional Learning. (2003). *Safe and sound: An educational leader's guide to evidence-based social and emotional learning (SEL) programs* (Illinois ed.). Accessed at http://static1.squarespace.com/static/513f79f9e4b05ce7b70e9673/t/5331c141e4b0fba62007694a/1395769665836/safe-and-sound-il-edition.pdf on April 7, 2016.

Coloroso, B. (1994). *Kids are worth it!: Giving your child the gift of inner discipline*. New York: William Morrow.

Cromwell, S. (2002). Is your school's culture toxic or positive? *Education World*, *6*(2). Accessed at www.educationworld.com/a_admin/admin/admin275.shtml on April 7, 2016.

Darling-Hammond, L. (2003). Keeping good teachers: Why it matters, what leaders can do. *Educational Leadership*, *60*(8), 6–13.

Deci, E. L., & Ryan, R. M. (2000). The "what" and "why" of goal pursuits: Human needs and the self-determination of behavior. *Psychological Inquiry, 11*(4), 227–268.

DuFour, R., DuFour, R., Eaker, R., Many, T., & Mattos, M. (2016). *Learning by doing: A handbook for Professional Learning Communities at Work* (3rd ed.). Bloomington, IN: Solution Tree Press.

Dweck, C. S. (2006). *Mindset: The new psychology of success.* New York: Ballantine Books.

Edmonds, R. (1979). Effective schools for the urban poor. *Educational Leadership, 37*(1), 15–18, 20–24.

Elmore, R. F. (2004). *School reform from the inside out: Policy, practice, and performance.* Cambridge, MA: Harvard Education Press.

Engels, K. (2015). What teachers know that computers don't. *Educational Leadership, 73*(3), 72–76.

Erkens, C. (2016). *Collaborative common assessments: Teamwork. Instruction. Results.* Bloomington, IN: Solution Tree Press.

Finlayson, M. (2009, July). The impact of teacher absenteeism on student performance: The case of the Cobb County School District. *Dissertations, Theses and Capstone Projects*, Paper 4. Accessed at http://digitalcommons .kennesaw.edu/cgi/viewcontent.cgi?article=1006&context=etd on April 7, 2016.

Frankl, V. E. (2006). *Man's search for meaning.* Boston: Beacon Press.

Freitas, F. A., & Leonard, L. J. (2011). Maslow's hierarchy of needs and student academic success. *Teaching and Learning in Nursing, 6*(1), 9–13.

Fullan, M. (2005). *Leadership and sustainability: System thinkers in action.* San Francisco: Corwin Press.

Fullan, M., & Quinn, J. (2016). *Coherence: The right drivers in action for schools, districts, and systems.* Thousand Oaks, CA: Corwin Press.

Fullan, M., & St. Germain, C. (2006). *Learning places: A field guide for improving the context of schooling.* Thousand Oaks, CA: Corwin Press.

Ginott, H. G. (1972). *Teacher and child: A book for parents and teachers.* New York: Macmillan.

Goleman, D. (2006). *Social intelligence: The new science of human relationships.* New York: Bantam Books.

Gregory, A., & Weinstein, R. S. (2004). Connection and regulation at home and in school: Predicting growth in achievement for adolescents. *Journal of Adolescent Research, 19*(4), 405–427.

Guskey, T. R. (2003). How classroom assessments improve learning. *Educational Leadership, 60*(5). Accessed at www.ascd.org/publications/educational -leadership/feb03/vol60/num05/How-Classroom-Assessments-Improve -Learning.aspx on April 7, 2016.

Hamre, B. K., & Pianta, R. C. (2005). Can instructional and emotional support in the first-grade classroom make a difference for children at risk of school failure? *Child Development, 76*(5), 949–967.

Harris, M. J., & Rosenthal, R. (1985). Mediation of interpersonal expectancy effects: 31 meta-analyses. *Psychological Bulletin, 97*(3), 363–386.

Hattie, J. (2009). *Visible learning: A synthesis of over 800 meta-analyses relating to achievement.* New York: Routledge.

Hattie, J. (2012). *Visible learning for teachers: Maximizing impact on learning.* New York: Routledge.

Hattie, J., & Timperley, H. (2007). The power of feedback. *Review of Educational Research, 77*(1), 81–112.

Hattie, J., & Yates, G. (2014). *Visible learning and the science of how we learn.* New York: Routledge.

Hawken, L. S. (2006). School psychologists as leaders in the implementation of a targeted intervention: The behavior education program. *School Psychology Quarterly, 21*(1), 91–111.

Hawkins, J. D., Catalano, R. F., Kosterman, R., Abbott, R., & Hill, K. G. (1999). Preventing adolescent health-risk behaviors by strengthening protection during childhood. *Archives of Pediatrics and Adolescent Medicine, 153*(3), 226–234.

Heacox, D. (2014). *Differentiating instruction in the regular classroom: How to reach and teach all learners, grades K–12.* Minneapolis, MN: Free Spirit.

Hierck, T. (2009). Differentiated pathways to success. In T. R. Guskey (Ed.), *The teacher as assessment leader* (pp. 249–262). Bloomington, IN: Solution Tree Press.

Hierck, T., Coleman, C., & Weber, C. (2011). *Pyramid of behavior interventions: Seven keys to a positive learning environment.* Bloomington, IN: Solution Tree Press.

Hierck, T., & Weber, C. (2014a). *RTI is a verb*. Thousand Oaks, CA: Corwin Press.

Hierck, T., & Weber, C. (2014b). *RTI roadmap for school leaders: Plan and go*. Englewood, CO: Lead + Learn Press.

Individuals With Disabilities Education Act of 2004, 1 U.S.C., § 601–682 (2004).

Jones, D. E., Greenberg, M., & Crowley, M. (2015). Early social-emotional functioning and public health: The relationship between kindergarten social competence and future wellness. *American Journal of Public Health, 105*(11), 2283–2290.

Karnes, F. A., & Chauvin, J. C. (2000). *Leadership development program*. Scottsdale, AZ: Gifted Psychology Press.

Kise, J. A. G. (2014). *Unleashing the positive power of differences: Polarity thinking in our schools*. Thousand Oaks, CA: Corwin Press.

Kohn, A. (1996). *Beyond discipline: From compliance to community*. Alexandria, VA: Association for Supervision and Curriculum Development.

Kottler, J. A., & Zehm, S. J. (1993). *On being a teacher: The human dimension*. Thousand Oaks, CA: Corwin Press.

Kouzes, J. M., & Posner, B. Z. (2010). *The truth about leadership: The no-fads, heart-of-the-matter facts you need to know*. San Francisco: Jossey-Bass.

Krueger, P. M., Tran, M. K., Hummer, R. A., & Chang, V. W. (2015). Mortality attributable to low levels of education in the United States. *PLOS ONE, 10*(7). Accessed at http://journals.plos.org/plosone/article?id=10.1371/journal.pone.0131809 on April 7, 2016.

Lally, P., van Jaarsveld, C. H. M., Potts, H. W. W., & Wardle, J. (2010). How are habits formed: Modelling habit formation in the real world. *European Journal of Social Psychology, 40*(6), 998–1009.

Lewis, T. (2007). *Environmental inventory*. Handout presented at the Making Connections conference, Richmond, British Columbia, Canada.

March, R. E., & Horner, R. H. (2002). Feasibility and contributions of functional behavioral assessment in schools. *Journal of Emotional and Behavioral Disorders, 10*(3), 158–170.

Marzano, R. J. (2003). *What works in schools: Translating research into action*. Alexandria, VA: Association for Supervision and Curriculum Development.

Miller, R. (2001, November). *Greater expectations to improve student learning* [Report]. Washington, DC: Association of American Colleges and Universities. Accessed at www.greaterexpectations.org/briefing_papers/ImproveStudentLearning.html on April 7, 2016.

Miller, R. T., Murnane, R. J., & Willett, J. B. (2008). Do teacher absences impact student achievement?: Longitudinal evidence from one urban school district. *Educational Evaluation and Policy Analysis, 30*(2), 181–200.

National Center for Education Statistics. (2001, November). *Dropout rates in the United States: 2000* (NCES 2002-114). Washington, DC: U.S. Department of Education, Office of Educational Research and Improvement.

National Scientific Council on the Developing Child. (2015). *Supportive relationships and active skill-building strengthen the foundations of resilience* (Working Paper No. 13). Cambridge, MA: Center on the Developing Child at Harvard University. Accessed at http://developingchild.harvard.edu/wp-content/uploads/2015/05/The-Science-of-Resilience.pdf on April 7, 2016.

Ng'andu, J., Price, O. A., & Baron, W. (2015, December 22). *Lifelong success starts with social-emotional learning* [Blog Post]. Accessed at www.edutopia.org/blog/lifelong-success-starts-with-sel-ngandu-price-baron on December 30, 2015.

Nuthall, G. (2007). *The hidden lives of learners.* Wellington: New Zealand Council for Educational Research Press.

Patty, W. L., & Johnson, L. S. (1953). *Personality and adjustment.* New York: McGraw-Hill.

Reeves, D. (2000). *Accountability in action: A blueprint for learning organizations.* Denver: Advanced Learning Press.

Reeves, D. (2001). *101 questions and answers about standards, assessment, and accountability.* Denver: Advanced Learning Press.

Reeves, D. (2003). *High performance in high poverty schools: 90/90/90 and beyond.* Denver: Center for Performance Assessment.

Reeves, D. (2005). Putting it all together: Standards, assessment, and accountability in successful professional learning communities. In R. DuFour, R. Eaker, & R. DuFour (Eds.), *On common ground: The power of professional learning communities* (pp. 45–63). Bloomington, IN: Solution Tree Press.

Reeves, D. (2009). Looking deeper into the data. *Educational Leadership, 66*(4), 89–90.

Resnick, M. D., Bearman, P. S., Blum, R. W., Bauman, K. E., Harris, K. M., Jones, J., et al. (1997). Protecting adolescents from harm: Findings from the National Longitudinal Study on Adolescent Health. *Journal of the American Medical Association, 278*(10), 823–832.

Rodriguez, V. (2014). *The teaching brain: An evolutionary trait at the heart of education.* New York: New Press.

Roorda, D. L., Koomen, H. M. Y., Spilt, J. L., & Oort, F. J. (2011). The influence of affective teacher–student relationships on students' school engagement and achievement: A meta-analytic approach. *Review of Educational Research, 81*(4), 493–529.

Ryan, R. M., & Deci, E. L. (2000). Self-determination theory and the facilitation of intrinsic motivation, social development, and well-being. *American Psychologist, 55*(1), 68–78.

Schilling, K. M., & Schilling, K. L. (1999). Increasing expectations for student effort. *About Campus, 4*(2), 4–10.

Schimmer, T. (2016). *Grading from the inside out: Bringing accuracy to student assessment through a standards-based mindset.* Bloomington, IN: Solution Tree Press.

Shifrer, D. (2013). Stigma of a label: Educational expectations for high school students labeled with learning disabilities. *Journal of Health and Social Behavior, 54*(4), 462–480.

Thompson, J. G. (1998). *Discipline survival kit for the secondary teacher.* West Nyack, NY: Center for Applied Research in Education.

Tomlinson, C. A. (2000). Reconcilable differences?: Standards-based teaching and differentiation. *Educational Leadership, 58*(1). Accessed at www.ascd.org /publications/educational_leadership/sept00/vol58/num01/Reconcilable _Differences%C2%A2_Standards-Based_Teaching_and_Differentiation.aspx on April 7, 2016.

Treffinger, D. J., & Sortore, M. R. (1992). *Programming for giftedness: A contemporary view.* Melbourne, FL: Center for Creative Learning.

Walker, H. M., Ramsey, E., & Gresham, F. M. (2004). *Antisocial behavior in school: Evidence-based practices* (2nd ed.). Belmont, CA: Wadsworth.

Whitaker, T. (2012). *Shifting the monkey: The art of protecting good people from liars, criers, and other slackers.* Bloomington, IN: Solution Tree Press.

Williams, K. C., & Hierck, T. (2015). *Starting a movement: Building culture from the inside out in professional learning communities.* Bloomington, IN: Solution Tree Press.

Wright, J. (2014). *Strategies for struggling learners in the era of CCSS and RTI.* Naples, FL: National Professional Resources.

Zins, J. E., & Elias, M. J. (2006). Social and emotional learning. In G. G. Bear & K. M. Minke (Eds.), *Children's needs III: Development, prevention, and intervention* (pp. 1–13). Bethesda, MD: National Association of School Psychologists.

INDEX

A

ABC direct-observation tool, 66–69, 78
assessments
    See also data-driven decisions
    of evidence, 76–79
assignments, routine when turning in,
    30–31
at-risk students, 42

B

Bag of Me strategy, 36
Baird, B., 12
Baron, W., 101–102
Becker, W. C., 51
behavior, causes of, 110
behavioral challenges, strategies for
    addressing, 79–86
behavioral expectations, teaching, 36–39
Behavior Education Program (BEP),
    83–84
behavior pyramid, description of, 4–5
Blackwell, L., 23
Bloom's taxonomy, 13, 35–36, 99
Buffum, A., 85

C

Chang, V. W., 15
chase time, 25–26
Check-In Check-Out (CICO), 83
class meetings, 31–32

classroom culture
    beliefs needed for creating, 8, 9
    defined, 7
    example, 10–11
    teacher-student relationships, role of
        positive, 11–16
classroom expectations
    aligning beliefs with, 22–24
    common language, need for, 21
    description of, 19–33
    modeling, 21, 26
    reviewing, 39–41
    routines, establishing, 27–32
    rules versus, 20–22
    setting up, 24–26
    struggling students, working with,
        32–33
    student involvement in establishing,
        26–27
    teaching, 36–39
Coleman, C., 1, 4, 46
collaboration
    cautions for, 96–99
    compliance versus commitment,
        92–94
    developing role of, 91–92
    parents and, 97–99
    purpose of, 97
    student, 99–103
Collaborative for Academic, Social, and
    Emotional Learning (CASEL), 99–100

Pyramid of Behavior Interventions
Tom Hierck, Charlie Coleman, and Chris Weber
Students thrive when educators hold high expectations for behavior as well as academics. This book shows how to use a three-tiered pyramid of behavior supports to create a school culture and classroom climates in which learning is primed to occur.
BKF532

Transformative Teaching
Kathleen Kryza, MaryAnn Brittingham, and Alicia Duncan
Examine the most effective strategies for leading diverse students to develop the skills they need inside and outside the classroom. By understanding and exploring students' emotional, cultural, and academic needs, educators will be better prepared to help all students become lifelong learners.
BKF623

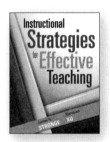

Instructional Strategies for Effective Teaching
James H. Stronge and Xianxuan Xu
Discover research-based instructional strategies teachers, coaches, and administrators can use to enhance their everyday practices. Organized around ten methods of instruction, this user-friendly guide will help you dig deep into classroom discussion, concept mapping, inquiry-based learning, and more.
BKF641

Thriving as a New Teacher
John F. Eller and Sheila A. Eller
Discover strategies and tools for new-teacher success. Explore the six critical areas related to teaching that most impact new teachers and their students, from understanding yourself and implementing effective assessments to working confidently and effectively with colleagues.
BKF661

Solution Tree | Press   *a division of*
Solution Tree

Visit SolutionTree.com or call 800.733.6786 to order.

Wait! Your professional development journey doesn't have to end with the last pages of this book.

We realize improving student learning doesn't happen overnight. And your school or district shouldn't be left to puzzle out all the details of this process alone.

No matter where you are on the journey, we're committed to helping you get to the next stage.

Take advantage of everything from **custom workshops** to **keynote presentations** and **interactive web and video conferencing**. We can even help you develop an action plan tailored to fit your specific needs.

Let's get the conversation started.

Call 888.763.9045 today.

SolutionTree.com